BRUSSELS

BRUGES | GHENT | LILLE

CONTENTS

Published by Thomas Cook Publishing
PO Box 227, Thorpe Wood
Peterborough PE3 6PU
United Kingdom

E–mail: books@thomascook.com

Text: © The Thomas Cook Group Ltd 2000
Maps: © The Thomas Cook Group Ltd 2000
Transport map: © TCS 2000

ISBN 1 841570 346

Distributed in the United States of America by the Globe Pequot Press,
PO Box 480, Guilford, Connecticut 06437, USA.

Distributed in Canada by Whitecap Books, 351 Lynn Avenue,
North Vancouver, British Columbia, Canada V7J 2C4.

Distributed in Australia and New Zealand by Peribo Pty Limited,
58 Beaumont Road, Mt Kuring-Gai, NSW, 2080, Australia.

Publisher: Stephen York
Commissioning Editor: Deborah Parker
Map Editor: Bernard Horton

Series Editor: Christopher Catling

Written and researched by: Andrew Sanger

Cover photograph: Alex Kouprianoff

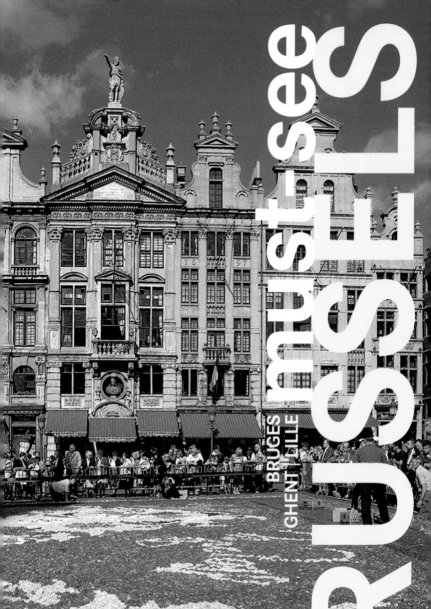

must-see

BRUSSELS

BRUGES | GHENT | LILLE

ANDREW SANGER

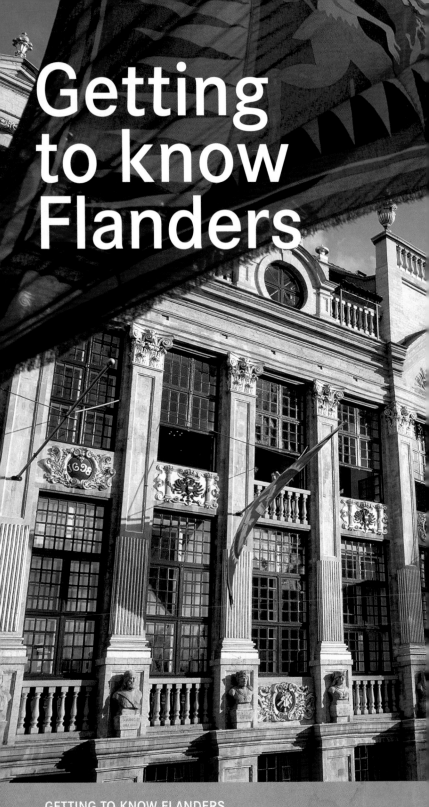

Getting
to know
Flanders

Discovering Flanders

Flanders has been reborn. Have a think about it over some breakfast waffles and a strong, creamy coffee, or a glass of lambic beer, at one of the exuberantly decorated old bars in the centre of Brussels.

Past power

As capital of old Flanders, Brussels has long been one of the great cities of Europe, admired for style, riches, art and culture. In the past, the Flemish were found everywhere – from Spain and North Africa to the court of the Russian Tsar. They were the most skilled of artisans, the greatest of artists, the most enterprising and industrious of traders and merchants. The Flemish language was once as internationally important as French and English are now. Drop into any of the city's museums and churches to find a treasure trove of Flemish art of the golden-age, from gorgeous old tapestries and the meticulous canvases of the **Flemish Primitives** to the more fantastic allegorical visions of **Brueghel** and **Hieronymus Bosch**.

Flemish survival

As time passed, and empires waxed and waned, Flanders fell under the knife of history. Finally carved up and divided into Holland, Belgium and northern France, it was all but forgotten as a region and a culture.

Yet, despite everything, the Flemish have remained utterly Flemish. They have continued to speak their throat-scraping language, to brew their sharp, frothy beer, to listen to the endless melodic clink-clanking of their steeple bells and to remember their flamboyant heritage. At the same time, their capital became annoyingly French, which, on the plus side, gave it a more modern high society and new post-Revolutionary high ideals – not to mention *haute cuisine* and *haute couture*. Thanks to the new French intellectualism, radical ideas flourished.

The age of the train

At last, partly thanks to the European Union and partly to **Eurostar** (and **Thalys**, the high-speed link with Paris), Brussels has suddenly been rediscovered. This marvellous, unique mix of French and Flemish attitudes is as glorious as ever, gilded and grand, packed full of art and architecture, style and dignity and the quiet, civilised enjoyment of life.

Undoubtedly, Brussels and the other Flemish towns also have an obvious and immediate visual charm: canals, bikes bumping over cobbled squares, wildly decorative town halls, masses of flowers, elaborate spires and gables. Along with the picturesque, though, there's a quirkiness. The Flemish, it appears, have an eye for the bizarre, the comic and absurd.

How else to explain why so many Surrealists were Belgian? **Giant Festivals**, where parades and processions are led by gigantic, grotesque figures, literally 'model citizens', or where mock battles take place between contestants on stilts, show that this love of strange symbolism and eccentricity runs deep. It's expressed too by the **Art Nouveau** doorways, balconies and frescoes, and in today's street art, cartoon-strip murals and, perhaps, in the city's extraordinary mascot and symbol of defiance – the **Mannekin Pis**. That cheeky little chappie, dressed in a succession of totally unlikely miniature outfits, cheerfully and proudly showers his contempt on all invaders – foreigners and would-be conquerors – and perhaps even on the very Eurocrats who have put Brusssels so firmly back on the world map.

A day in the life of Brussels

It's not obvious that Brussels has problems. To outsiders, the city presents an image of perfect peace and prosperity and a wholehearted (but respectable) enjoyment of the good things in life. True, the traffic is bad and the driving fast and furious, but at least the cars are often in the luxury class.

Under that placid exterior, the whole of Belgium is riven by long-standing divides and dissent. The language riots of the 1960s may be over, but the mutual distrust between Flemish speakers and French speakers (Walloons) remains intense.

Bridges and chasms

The national motto, 'Unity is strength', is more of a pious hope than a reality. At the moment, this nation, which symbolises the European dream of unity, is itself coming apart at the seams. **Wallonia** (the southeast of the country) and **Flanders** have separate regional governments, which are becoming increasingly autonomous.

The capital city, meanwhile, has become a separate self-governing region with a rapidly declining population – now under 1 million. What is more, one-third of those resident in Brussels are now foreign. Outsiders, Belgians grumble, have brought crime, high prices and a housing crisis to Brussels.

There are other terrible, unbridgeable gulfs. In Belgium, it's a case of 'Don't mention the War'. The large number of Nazi collaborators, mainly Flemish, has been a running sore in Belgium ever since World War II ended. As recently as 1996, the trial of an accused wartime collaborator led to wide-ranging protests – both for and against the process of raking up the past .

Worse, there are much more menacing, immediate concerns. The discovery that Marc Dutroux, paedophile and child murderer, had friends in high places (and at the local police station) led to nationwide outrage. The ensuing investigations revealed a nightmare of incompetence, corruption, racism and clandestine fascism among officials.

The sunnier side

How can such a tiny land bear so much scandal and downright evil? The answer, oddly, is that the initial impression of contentment is close to the truth. All can be forgotten if one concentrates on eating, drinking and having a good time. Away from the tourist haunts, take a look at the crowds of cheerful shoppers, snackers and browsers in real-life Brussels – in Avenue Louise, Galerie Louise and Galerie de la Toison d'Or, or at busy Porte de Namur. Whatever the problems may be, exaggerated or not, it seems Belgians are united in their love of Belgium, shopping and the enjoyment of life!

Despite their sweet tooth and a legendary fondness for **french fries and mayonnaise**, Belgians are also serious diners. With a passion for hearty traditional dishes, well prepared and served in generous portions, the love of fine cooking is no mere cliché. Brussels enjoys more **Michelin-rated restaurants** per head than Paris, not to mention 100 different breweries making some 600 types of **beer**, and a bewildering plethora of high-class confectioners, fine patisseries and delicatessens.

Yesterday and tomorrow

Known as 'the cockpit of Europe', Belgium for centuries was the battleground for history-making conflicts. Now it hopes to be the cockpit in another sense: the driving seat from which Europe's future is decided peacefully.

Basic divisions within the country started early, when the Romans colonised the southern territory of the Belgii tribe, while leaving the northern stretches Germanic. Flanders first appeared on the map just over 1000 years ago, simply as a buffer zone between the Kingdom of France and the German Empire.

Wool and nobility

This inauspicious, in-between position determined the whole destiny of the country. Trading with England, France and Germany, its towns and settlements took up the high-quality wool weaving which laid the foundation of Flanders' enormous prosperity. On 11 July 1302 the Flemish citizens thrashed the French at the **Battle of the Golden Spurs**: still celebrated as the Flemish national holiday. By the end of the 14th century, weddings joined this vulnerable land to the **Duchy of Burgundy**, under whose patronage Flemish artists and craftsmen acquired unrivalled skill and excellence.

Although their own home was in Dijon, the **Dukes of Burgundy** made Brussels their capital. When Mary of Burgundy married Maximilian of Austria, and their son Philip married Joanna, daughter of the King of Spain, a huge empire was formed. In 1500, Philip and Joanna's son Charles was born in Ghent, then one of the wealthiest towns in the world. As **Holy Roman Emperor, Charles V**, he inherited the whole of Flanders, Spain and the Austrian Empire, not to mention all their newly-acquired colonies in America and Asia. Charles' capital was Brussels.

Religion and revolution

But that sumptuous period was soon to end. Charles abdicated, his empire broke up, Belgium came under Spanish and then Austrian rule, and war broke out between Protestants and Catholics. Gradually, once-rich Flemish towns sank into decline. France, after destroying the Grand Place, went to war with Austria for possession of Flanders. Inspired by the **French Revolution**, the Belgian people wanted independence. But it was not until 1830 that the Brussels Revolution won the Belgians their long-desired independence. Leopold I of Saxe-Coburg-Gotha was crowned as the new country's first king. Two world wars soon proved that Belgium, easily beaten and occupied by the Germans, could not survive on its own. After World War II, Belgium keenly supported European co-operation. In 1957 Brussels became capital of the new **European Economic Community**, forerunner of today's European Union.

Peace in Europe

Time has moved on. Belgium, for all its love of tradition, has pinned its colours to a European future. Ironically, old divisions inside the country resurfaced. For the country's Flemish majority – two-thirds of Belgium's population – it still rankles that their capital city is predominantly French. Belgians are puzzled about where increasing regional autonomy may lead: will Flanders and Wallonia split altogether? Perhaps in a new unified Europe of Regions, that would not matter so much.

People and places

Imagine life without the saxophone – no blues, no rock, no swing or big band sounds! The world would be a poorer, drabber place without this magnificent invention, the creation of Belgian Adolphe Sax (1814–94) whose raucous new instrument (patented in 1845) changed the look, as well as the sound, of music.

The old flamboyant Flemish love of art, architecture, creativity and decoration lives on in modern Belgium. The country adores music, theatre and art. Music festivals, concerts and events take place all year round without pause. Not just classical music, in which the country excels, but especially jazz. The best-known Belgian among jazz buffs is the great **Toots Thielemans**, master of harmonica, but there have been many others, including drummer **Bruno Castellucci**, guitarist **René Thomas** and saxophonist **Jacques Pelzer**. Jazz struck a chord with the people of Belgium even before the war, and now all its cities have clubs and bars where you can hear exciting new jazz names.

Performing arts

The city has dozens of theatre companies, and opera, too, is thriving here: Brussels' prestigious **Théâtre Royal de la Monnaie** is a leading European venue for classical and modern stage events.

Above all, **contemporary dance** is Brussels' forte. An astounding number of dance companies – over 50 in all – are established in the city. Most distinguished of them is Anne Teresa de Keersmaeker's company, **Rosas**. Herself one of the world's leading modern choreographers, de Keersmaeker is one of the most exciting members of a young generation of Belgian experimentalists in the arts. Favouring a stark, minimalist style, and a distinctive combination of spoken word, film, music and dance, De Keersmaeker began choreographing in 1980, when she left

Maurice Bejart's acclaimed Mudra dance school in Brussels. Her work has won awards all around the globe. The most admired piece, *Fase*, with music by modern young Belgian composers Theirry De Mey and Peter Vermeersch, won New York's prestigious 'Bessie Award'. De Keersmaeker is now an artist in residence at Théâtre de la Monnaie.

Catwalk style

Brussels is also the home of several modern fashion designers. Again there seems to be a well-defined Belgian style, rooted in quirky simplicity and minimalism. Beside the local talent, many other young European designers have set up shop here. Take a look in the shopfronts along Rue Antoine Dansaert and around Avenue Louise. Sought-after local designer Gerald Watelet is here, and Olivier Strelli (as worn by Mick Jagger), and young designer Kaat Tilley.

Surrealists and bureaucrats

Despite these high-fliers in their field, most of the really famous Belgians seem to have died a few years ago. Victor Horta, the Art Nouveau innovator of the 1890s, and Surrealist painters Magritte and Delvaux (who died in 1994, aged nearly 100), are among outstanding Bruxellois of the 20th century. Today, important and powerful people in Brussels are more often faceless than famous. EU officials, like former president Jacques Santer (actually from Luxembourg), are perhaps the individuals most associated with the city.

Then there's Tintin, the most famous Belgian in the world. Like the second-most famous, Agatha Christie's detective Hercule Poirot, he is fictitious. Tintin, though, has a life of his own, and has sparked a whole cartoon-strip mania in Belgium – so much so that Brussels now considers itself Europe's capital of the strip cartoon.

Getting around

Eurostar

Eurostar travellers arrive in Lille at Lille-Europe station, 10 minutes' walk from central Grand-Place. Eurostar then continues into Brussels, terminating at Gare du Midi, on the south side of the city centre. The Eurostar ticket is valid for local trains from Gare du Midi to Gare Centrale, 5 minutes by foot from Grand-Place and the city centre.

Belgian trains

Trains are quick, reliable, comfortable and inexpensive. A very frequent service connects Brussels to Bruges throughout the day, with a journey time of 55 minutes. Most of these trains stop at Ghent, 30 minutes from Brussels. *SNCB enquiries: 02 203 2880/203 3640.*

Buses, trams and the metro

For travelling between towns, buses represent a poor option compared to trains. In town, though, buses and trams are safe, clean, fast and inexpensive, and drivers generally speak some English. Brussels also has a small metro network, and stations are easy to spot with their large letter M. Another resource is Brussels' 'underground tram' (where ordinary trams run in tunnels). All public transport within a town is integrated and run by a single authority. A ticket for bus, tram or metro must be stamped on boarding and is valid for an hour.

Sightseeing in Bruges, Ghent and Lille is concentrated within a small, walkable area, but you may want to use the excellent bus services, or Lille's interesting, fully automated metro system (known as VAL) to get into the centre from Bruges or Ghent stations.

Taxis

Taxis, identified by a light on the roof, are metered and can be hailed in the street or picked up at cab ranks. The two main cab ranks in Bruges are the Markt square and the railway station. You can also phone for a taxi (a couple of useful Brussels numbers to note are *02 268 0000* and *02 349 4949*; in Bruges, call *050 334444* or *050 384660*). There's no need to tip, by the way – it's already included in the fare.

Bicycles

Locals love cycling and you might agree that it is an ideal way to get around, especially in Bruges. All railway stations rent bikes, as do many small private companies. Get details about renting from a railway station or tourist office.

Canalboats and riverboats

One of the best ways to get an overview of Bruges is on the popular canalboat tours. These can be boarded at Dijver, Huidenvettersplein, Vismarkt and other points: buy tickets on the spot. Canal tours generally run from March to October only, with a more infrequent schedule in winter months. A paddle-steamer also travels up and down the canal to Damme from Bruges, making a leisurely and enjoyable excursion.

Horsedrawn buggies

In Bruges, horsedrawn cabs are a popular and affordable way to tour the town or take a trip from Burg to the Begijnhof, or out as far as Damme. Their main pick-up point is Burg square.

Travel passes

If you plan to use Brussels' public transport a lot, a good option is to buy a *carnet* of either 5 or 10 tickets, or a 12-hour unlimited ticket. The Brussels tourist office also sells a one-day Tourist Pass giving unlimited travel and discounts to museums. Bruges, Ghent and Lille also have one-day unlimited travel passes.

For getting around the country, Belgian Railways (SNCB) offer a variety of cut-price ticket offers, Eurodomino rail rovers and discount passes for under 26s, over 60s, and small groups. Belgian rail tickets can often be bought in the UK, together with your Eurostar ticket.

Car hire

All the major international car rental companies have desks at Brussels airport and in the city.

Driving

Drive on the right and always give way to anything approaching from the right – even from minor roads and side turns. This rule, known as *priorité à droite*, may take the unwary by surprise in town centres, where traffic emerging from side roads will drive out – sometimes at high speed – even if you are on the main road.

Exceptions to the rule are: where your road has *passage protégé* (indicated by a rectangular yellow sign), where vehicles coming from the right are emerging from private property, or where other signs indicate that you have priority.

Belgian speed limits are generally 50kph (31mph) in town, 90kph (55 mph) out of town and 120kph (74mph) on dual carriageways and motorways. In France, the limit is normally 110kph (68mph) on dual carriageways, and 130kph (80mph) on motorways (sometimes lower on toll-free motorways). Motorways often have a minimum speed limit of 80kph (49mph), which in France generally only applies to the fast lane.

New drivers (first 2 years) must keep to limits about 10kph lower than indicated. Most minor offences, including speeding, not stopping at a Stop sign, overtaking where forbidden and not wearing a seat belt, are punishable by an on-the-spot fine of around £100.

Guided tours

Guided tours on foot set out daily from the Brussels main tourist office, in Grand-Place, and are followed by a 3-hour bus tour of the city (*tel: 02 513 77440*).

Coach tours of Bruges set out daily from Markt and take about one hour. You do not need to book in advance. You can also go on a guided bicycle tour of Bruges (*tel: 050 34 37 09*).

Taxi drivers are keen to give guided tours. They charge no more than what is on the meter. The driver may not be a qualified guide – but it can still be an enjoyable way to see the sights.

Maps and information

Before you go

For Lille
French Tourist Office: *178 Piccadilly, London W1V 0AL. Tel: 0891 244123; fax: 0171 493 6594.*

For Brussels, Bruges and Ghent
Tourism Flanders-Brussels:
29 Princes Street, London W1R 7RG. Tel: 0171 458 0044.

When you're there

Brussels
Tourist Information Brussels:
Hôtel de Ville, Grand-Place.
Tel: 02 513 8940;
fax: 02 514 4538.

Bruges
VVV/Toerisme Brugge: *Burg 11.*
Tel: 050 44 86 86; fax: 050 44 86 00.

Ghent
VVV/Toerisme Gand: *In the Belfry,*
Botermarkt. Tel: 09 266 5252;
fax: 09 225 6288.

Lille
Office de Tourisme:
Palais Rihour,
Place Rihour.
Tel: 03 20 21 94 21;
fax: 03 20 21 94 20.

Don't miss

1 Grand-Place, Brussels

Hang around in one of Europe's grandest city squares. Have a coffee and pastry at an outdoor table and admire the lavish, gilded buildings of the medieval Trade Guilds. **Pages 22–35**

2 Mannekin Pis, Brussels

Give the naughty little boy a few minutes of your time. Push through the crowds of gawpers and check out what he's wearing today. **Pages 40–41**

3 Royal Art Museums, Brussels

Get a quick grasp of what the great, classic Flemish painting was all about, and at the same time discover the vital contribution of Belgian painters to Surrealism. **Pages 64–65**

4 Cartoon-strip Brussels

As well as an excellent Cartoon-strip Centre, there's a trail of eye-catching cartoon murals through city centre streets.
Pages 52–53

5 Atomium, Brussels

This gigantic but perfectly proportioned model of an iron molecule stands 102m high and once symbolised the modern Brussels, though now it has the feel of an amusement park attraction – impressive, all the same. **Page 80**

6 Mini-Europe, Brussels

Incredibly, the real thing is only 25 times larger. Walk among perfect scale buildings and townscapes representing every country in the European Union. **Pages 80–81**

7 Markt and Burg, Bruges

Brussels, Ghent, Lille and Bruges seem to be all about inspiringly pretty squares, though none can beat these two for atmosphere, charm and set-piece Flemish architecture.
Pages 92–97

8 Canalside Bruges

Here's picture-book Belgium, thrillingly beautiful gabled stone houses reflected in the shimmering dark water. Walk alongside, or take a canal cruise. **Pages 108–115**

9 St Michielsbrug (St Michael's Bridge), Ghent

This lovely bridge at the heart of the town gives heart-stopping views of historic Ghent. **Page 129**

10 Vieux Lille

Wander and window shop along the cobbled lanes of Old Flanders in the heart of the modern city.
Pages 144-145

Brussels: Grand-Place

You walk into Grand-Place like a child into a drawing-room. Breathtaking on first sight, this is one of the most glorious public squares in Europe, or in the world. Enclosed by deliriously grandiose baroque 17th-century guildhalls, visitors gaze in wonder, as market stalls spread flowers and crisply smart waiters serve at neat brasserie tables perched on the cobbles.

BRUSSELS: Grand-Place

BRUSSELS: Grand-Place

Brussels: Grand-Place

*Getting there: **Metro:** The nearest metro stations are Bourse/Beurs and Gare Centrale/Centraal Station. **Trams:** Tramlines 23, 52, 55, 56 and 81 pass close by (Stop: Bourse or Grand-Place). **Train:** Gare Centrale/Centraal Station is a few minutes' walk away from Grand-Place.*

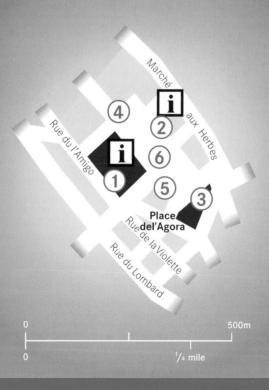

① Hôtel de Ville / Stadhuis (Town Hall)

Most magnificent of all the opulent architectural masterpieces in the Grand-Place, the elaborate, statue-encrusted Gothic Town Hall is the one with a massive, off-centre tower. Dating from the 1400s, it's several centuries older than the others, being the only building to survive the French bombardment of 1695. The main tourist office is here, with its own entrance onto Grand-Place.

Pages 26–27

② Maison du Roi / Broodhuis

Oddly, this palace facing the Town Hall was never a royal home, but it did belong to the Dukes of Burgundy and so passed to a local lad, the Emperor Charles V. The Flemish name reveals that it actually stands on the site of the former medieval Bakery Market. It's one of the grandest buildings in the Place.

Pages 28–29

③ Dukes of Brabant Hall

Taking up the whole southeastern side of the square, this mansion is named after the first-floor statuary, rather than for any connection with the real Dukes of Brabant. Topped with a handsome dome, the Dukes of Brabant Hall, in fact, comprises the guildhalls of several trades.

Page 31

④ Sit at a café

Call them touristy, but the stylish cafés and bars around the edge of the Grand-Place give the best possible view of the square – and the interiors give a unique glimpse of the splendour and wealth of the guilds. Unlike almost any other square anywhere, outdoor tables are set within smart enclosures.

Page 32

⑤ Brussels City Museum

Located inside the King of Spain Hall, one of the most astonishing exhibits in this unusual museum is the wardrobe of the Mannekin Pis, a collection of hundreds of tailor-made outfits.

Page 29

⑥ Flower Market

All day, every day. Wander slowly among the dazzling displays of colour as hundreds of flowering plants are set out below the gilded mansions, a reminder that the Grand-Place is essentially a market-place.

As well as a daily flower market, Grand-Place has its strange *Bird Market* every Sunday, at which amateurs buy and sell their pigeons and other live birds (*Sun 0900–1300*).

Tourist information

The city's main tourist office is in the square, with its own entrance under the arcades of the Town Hall. *Hôtel de Ville, Grand-Place. Tel: 02 513 8940; fax: 02 514 4538.*

Grand-Place/Grote Markt

*The story of Grand-Place is the story of Belgium. The original Brussels lies beneath these cobbles, for here was the swampy place (*broek sella*) that gave the city its name. At first a fortress, then a market-place – which it has remained – gradually the square became the economic, political and social centre of the growing Flemish capital. In every mood the Belgian people converged on this square: in jubilation or despair, to celebrate, to riot and to dissent.*

Muddling along

Anyone today wanting to create the most beautiful public square in Europe would bring in planning consultants, designers, architects and artists, lawyers and accountants and engineers. They would devise a logo and employ a PR firm. They would seek sponsorship and commercial partners and try to make the project pay for itself.

That's not how it happened in Brussels. There was no plan, and no overall authority responsible for the work. The trade guilds simply acquired land around the square and, over the centuries, built their halls as lavishly as funds would allow. The Dukes of Burgundy, too, when they inherited the city, constructed their opulent mansion here. Gradually Brussels became the symbol of Flemish industry, talent and wealth, and Grand-Place became the symbol of Brussels.

Invasion and destruction

Then, in the 17th century, came disaster. The French decided to take control of Flanders. In August 1695, in their efforts to capture the city, the French bombarded the square to smithereens. Using the high belfry of the Town Hall as their target, the French poured cannon fire into the centre of Brussels. Ironically, the Town Hall itself was not hit; it was the only building in the square to survive intact. Part of the **Maison du Roi** and three shopfronts were also left standing. The rest of the Grand-Place was destroyed.

Such was the power and prosperity of the traders of Brussels that everything was rebuilt immediately, and even more ostentatiously, with an extravagance of statuary and ornament and gilding. Interestingly, the **Governor of Brussels**, appointed by the King of Spain, made the first-ever attempt at town planning when he tried to take control of the hasty no-expense-spared rebuilding. However, the guilds were stronger than he, and did as they wished. The result was the Grand-Place of today, for it has hardly changed since.

> *I have never before seen such a great fire, nor so much desolation, as that which I have seen in this town.*
>
> **Commander of the French artillery, M de Vigny, 15 August 1695**

Ultimately, the French were victorious – and they called this magnificent square the Grand-Place, or 'Great Square'. For the Flemish, it remains, as it has always been, their Grote Markt, or 'Main Market-place'.

BRUSSELS: Grand-Place

Hôtel de Ville/Stadhuis (Town Hall)

Grand-Place – or Grote Markt – was already a place of importance in the 14th century, with the guildhalls of the bread, cloth and meat trades already standing, when the city fathers ordered the demolition of some houses and the clearing of a space for the construction of a Town Hall beside the market-place.

In Flanders, civic buildings have tended to be elaborate and palatial, and even today the main landmark in Flemish towns is usually the belfry of the Town Hall. The **Town Hall** of Brussels was to outshine them all.

The foundation stone was laid in 1401, and one spring day the following year the masons started work on a Gothic masterpiece that was to take 57 years to complete. The last part of the work involved dismantling the new belfry and replacing it with an even taller, grander one! Architect **Jan van Ruysbroek** carried out the replacement, and created a marvel of Gothic tracery, with a square section supporting an octagonal section, and a spire of exquisitely carved stone as delicate and elegant as Brussels lace. On the very pinnacle was placed a gilded copper statue of the **Archangel Michael**, with rather cumbersome wings, slaying the devil with a vicious-looking sword.

Thrilling asymmetry

To ensure that the building could take the weight of the new tower, Van Ruysbroek took a gamble and placed it slightly off-centre. The story is that, on finally seeing his finished work, Van Ruysbroek was so dissatisfied by the asymmetrical appearance that he walked up the 400 steps to the top of his 96m-high creation, and threw himself from the belfry, dying in agony on the cobbles below.

To the modern eye though, the imbalance is thrilling and beautiful. The façade, generously daubed with gold paint and encrusted with statues, is astonishing. The **carvings** depict a multitude of human and divine scenes, witty, wicked and sometimes just plain weird. Look out for the one of monks eating and drinking, another of someone being dunked in liquid, and another of people stacking chairs. They are said to be reminders of the houses that originally stood on the site. Most of the sculptures, by the way, were copied and replaced in the last century; the originals are in the Brussels City Museum (*see page 29*).

Interior views

The interior can be visited by joining a guided tour. Highlights of the visit include the renovated **Grand Staircase** and the sumptuously decorated, self-important official meeting rooms, still used by councillors. The painting on the ceiling of the main **Council Chamber** represents a meeting of the gods. In the **Maximilian Chamber**, lovely old Flemish tapestries cover the walls. In the antechamber to the **Burgomaster's Office**, note the paintings by Van Moer showing central Brussels before the River Senne was covered over.

Guided tours: Sun 1215; Tue 1130 and 1515; Wed 1515. Admission: £.

" *I am dazzled by Brussels. Grand-Place is a marvel.* "

Victor Hugo (1802–85)

La Maison du Roi/ Broodhuis

The French name (The King's House) is just a poetic exaggeration, while the Flemish (Bread House) is far too down to earth. In truth this richly ornamented Grand-Place masterpiece, facing the Town Hall from across the square, was never the residence of any king or queen, though it looks grand enough to have served that purpose. The Maison du Roi started out as the Brussels administrative offices of the Dukes of Burgundy, the rulers of medieval Flanders.

The regal connection comes with the Holy Roman Emperor Charles V, Duke of Burgundy, Emperor of Germany and King of Spain, who was born in Ghent and raised in Brussels. In 1515 he had the **Dukes' House**, as it was then called, extensively enlarged and further embellished – although, since Charles was only a teenager at the time, it is more likely that his advisers and counsellors took the decision to build themselves a fine new corporate headquarters office.

The house underwent further dramatic changes in the 19th century, when city officials took the view that it was falling into disrepair. They had the building restored and redesigned, and added the arcades and tower which are such a distinctive feature of the Maison du Roi today.

And **Bread House**? Clinging to the prosaic, commercial origins of the site, the Flemish prefer to remember that the original Dukes' House itself replaced the town's Bread Market which had stood here for centuries. Perhaps they're still smarting from the change.

To see inside, visit the Brussels City Museum.

Musée de la Ville de Bruxelles/Museum van der Stad Brussel

Apr–Sept: Mon–Thur 1000–1230, 1330–1700, Sat–Sun 1000–1300. Rest of the year: Mon–Thur 1000–1300, 1330–1600, Sat–Sun 1000–1300. Admission: £.

Located inside the Maison du Roi, the Brussels City Museum sets out to tell the colourful story of the city through an eclectic mix of art, historical manuscripts, photography and folklore.

It is only a partial success – some displays are dull, and you do need to be a real enthusiast to work through the accompanying text. Even so, there are some fine and easy-to-admire old Flemish tapestries and paintings. The **Tapestry Room** is especially sumptuous. Look in the **Paintings and Altarpieces Room** for the famous work by Pieter Breugel the Elder, *The Wedding Procession*. There is a wealth of medieval sculpture, too. In the **Gothic** section, you'll find the original (and sometimes amusing) 14th- and 15th-century sculptures from the Town Hall façade.

In the **Porcelain Room** you will discover the not-widely-appreciated fact that Brussels was once the rival to Delft for top-quality glazed ceramics. In the museum's **Faience & Pewter** section, an impressive display shows the exquisite work produced in this field by local craftsmen.

The last – and most popular – room is on the top floor, where the entire wardrobe of the **Mannekin Pis** is on view. Originally intended to be naked, the amusing 'little boy' was given his first suit of clothes 300 years ago, in a spirit of humour, by the then Governor of Brussels, ruling the city on behalf of King Charles II of Spain. The gesture was repeated by other dignitaries, until it became the custom for all visiting heads of state to present the statue with an outfit. Celebrities have joined in too (he even has a mini-boater presented by Maurice Chevalier), and now the Mannekin Pis possesses over 600 different suits, most of them immaculately tailored.

The Guildhalls

Each of the guildhalls around Grand-Place is identified by a visual sign – generally some symbolic feature on the façade. Walking clockwise around the square from the Town Hall, start at the beautiful terrace on the northwest side of Grand-Place.

Haberdashers' Hall (*7 Grand-Place*) is known as Le Renard (The Fox). Search in vain for some sign on the façade or doorway to explain this. The reason turns out to be that the sculptor's name, de Vos, happened to mean 'the Fox' in Flemish. His sculptures and carvings cover the imaginative façade.

Boatmens' Hall, next door (*6 Grand-Place*), is known as Le Cornet (The Horn). Its façade is an even more imaginative departure from tradition, and the gable has been made to resemble a 17th-century ship.

Archers' Hall (*5 Grand-Place*), is called La Louve (The She-Wolf) because of a carving – again by Mr Fox! – of twins Romulus and Remus being suckled by a wolf.

The Cabinetmakers' and Coopers' Hall (*4 Grand-Place*), known as Le Sac (The Bag), is a riot of hallucinatory carving and imagery. The building's name comes from the weird

carving above the door, which shows a man thrusting his hands into a sack.

Tallow Merchants' Hall (*3 Grand-Place*), called La Brouette (The Wheelbarrow), has become a café. More controlled than its neighbours, the reliefs and carvings make an attractive façade.

Bakers' Hall (*1–2 Grand-Place*) has long been known as the **King of Spain Hall**. This, too, is now a café. With its lovely balustrade and octagonal dome, this is the most classical and Italianate of the guildhalls. Cross to the northeastern side of the square, largely taken

up by the **Maison du Roi** (*see pages 28–29*). Beyond it stands a house known as **La Chambrette d'Amman**, which once was the office of Brussels' Mayor and Magistrate (or 'Amman'), appointed by the Dukes of Brabant.

In **Painters' Hall** (*26–27 Grand-Place*), known as Le Pigeon, Victor Hugo rented a room in 1851, and is said to have written two plays during his stay. **Tailors' Hall** (*24 –25 Grand-Place*), more grandly called La Chaloupe d'Or (The Golden Sloop), now houses a café.

Cross to the square's southeastern terrace, taken up entirely by **Le Maison des Ducs de Brabant** (*13–19 Grand-Place*). This vast and imposing structure encloses the **Tanners' Hall** (known as La Fortune), the **Millers' Hall** (with its sign of The Windmill), the **Carpenters' Hall** (The Pewter Pot) and the **Stoneworkers' Hall** (La Colline – The Hill), as well as some private houses.

Cross again, to the little terrace in the square's southwestern corner. Here (*11–12 Grand-Place*) are two handsome private homes, **La Rose** and **Le Mont Thabor**. Next to them, **Brewers' Hall** (*10 Grand-Place*), better known as L'Arbre d'Or (The Golden Tree), is as richly ornamented as possible. Today it houses a fascinating **Brewery Museum** (*Apr–Sept: Mon–Thur 1000–1230, 1330–1700, Sat–Sun 1000–1300. Rest of the year: Mon–Thur 1000–1300, 1330–1600, Sat–Sun 1000–1300. Admission: £*).

Butchers' Hall (*9 Grand-Place*), better known as Le Cygne (The Swan), is now a smart restaurant. Karl Marx and Friedrich Engels, who lived in Brussels in the 1840s, held fortnightly Communist meetings in this house. Next door (*8 Grand-Place*), the last building before returning to the Town Hall, is the small private house, **L'Etoile** (The Star).

Eating and Drinking

Several old guildhalls have become bars or restaurants, giving an unrivalled view of the square, as well as the chance to see inside the buildings. Watch out, though, for high prices and unexpected extras in this tourist heartland. If you want more choice, step into the side streets (see pages 48–50).

La Chaloupe d'Or

24 Grand-Place. Tel: 511 41 61. Open 1000–0100 daily. ££. Most appealing of the Grand-Place bars, this former Tailors' Hall looks across the flower market to the Town Hall. Go upstairs for the best view.

La Maison du Cygne

9 Grand-Place. Tel: 511 82 44. Open for lunch and dinner. £££. Such a smart, pricey restaurant inside the former Hall of the Guild of Butchers ought to have a hearty menu, and so it does. This is now one of the most enjoyable eating places in Brussels, though a little full of lunchtime suits tucking into truffles, foie gras or oysters *au champagne*. The entrance is in Rue Charles Buls, beside the Town Hall.

La Rose Blanche

11 Grand-Place. Tel: 513 64 79. Open 1000–0100 or 0200 daily. ££. It's right next door to the Brewers' Guild Hall and the beer museum, so it seems right that this enjoyable brasserie serves an extensive range of beers. Decent food available too from lunchtime onwards.

Le Roy d'Espagne

1 Grand-Place. Tel: 513 08 07. Open 1000–0100 daily. ££. Nice address and nice location in the fabulously opulent King of Spain Hall (or the Bakers' Hall, if you prefer) with tip-top service provided by smart waiters in traditional long white aprons. It plays up the local colour and historic charm and attracts crowds of tourists, but is still a good place for a drink or a snack.

't Kelderke

6 Grand-Place. Tel: 513 73 44. Open 1200–0200 daily. ££. This popular lower-priced place has Belgian beers and specialities.

Which beer?

Tourists buying a beer tend to miss out on the literally hundreds of different kinds of local brews. The main distinctively Belgian types of beer are lambic, *which is naturally fermented (ie without yeast),* gueuze, *which is made of blended lambics, and the fruit lambics* Kriek *(cherry-flavoured) and* Framboise *(raspberry). Oh, and you need to know if you want a Trappist or abbey ale (which can be* Doubel *or* Tripel, *depending how large you like your drink), or a red, brown, amber or white ale. And then, there's the huge choice of brands – ask the waiter or barman for advice – they're proud to give it.*

Shopping

You can't take them home with you (unless you're leaving that day), so the daily flower market in the square is more a visual treat for tourists than a shopping opportunity. There are shops around the Place, mostly selling lace and souvenirs, but for these and other good buys you'd be better off looking in surrounding streets. Check that lace is genuinely Belgian and handmade, unless you are happy with the cheaper, and more usual, machine-made products.

Rubbrecht

23 Grand-Place. Tel: 512 0218. Attractive lace shop with huge range of pretty pieces, old and new handmade lace, large and small items, and all genuinely Belgian.

Godiva

22 Grand-Place. Tel: 511 2537. Open daily till midnight. One of the city's best chocolate shops, part of the well-known Belgian chain.

After dark

Romantic strollers and diners linger in the square or make their way here until late into the evening. Grand-Place is as beautiful at night as during the day, with spotlights playing on the guildhalls, the Maison du Roi and the Town Hall. Several bars and restaurants are open way past midnight, some with a disco atmosphere at night.

What are guilds?

In modern Belgium, many guilds (together with the more aristocratic confréries, *or 'brotherhoods') survive as highly ritualised closed societies. Their influence on society is hard to assess, but certainly they adore pageantry, and have done much to keep tradition alive.*

Trade origins

To understand the role played by Belgium's powerful guilds, think of the Freemasons. The international Masonic Brotherhood started as an exclusive order for genuine skilled stonemasons. Think, too, of the Livery Companies of the City of London (whose names, the Haberdashers, the Pewterers and the Merchant Taylors, show their humble trade origins). Like modern trades unions or professional organisations, the guilds originally existed to further the interests of their members, to protect and care for the workers of that particular trade, and to provide benefits in time of need.

Tradition and pageantry

Over centuries, and through the massive fortunes accumulated as a result of Flanders' commercial success, these humble workers' organisations have evolved to become the backbone of Belgium's powerful establishment. It's also partly because of the guilds that Belgium (and French Flanders too) are so vibrant with festivals and traditional

BRUSSELS: Grand-Place

events. Ceremonial hunts and marches, processions and feasts, and the strange **Giant Festivals** observed in so many Flemish towns and cities, are often organised by a traditional guild or brotherhood.

The Grand-Place in festive mood

Most of the gaudily decorated, gold-painted buildings all around the Grand-Place are still used by the historic local guilds, though their ceremonial and charitable functions are now considerably more prestigious than the proceedings of the medieval craft guilds out of which they evolved. If you are here at the right time you may witness the tables of Grand-Place suddenly pushed aside for a celebration, a fair, or a festival. The square holds dramatic and colourful events right though the year, in every season. None is grander than the medieval pageantry of the **Ommegang**, held every July, which celebrates the founding of the city, and whose organisation is still the preserve of an exclusive brotherhood.

Brussels:
The City's
Heart

The narrow cobbled streets, covered lanes and busy squares around Grand-Place have an infectious dynamism. Their mouthwatering names capture the down-to-earth, mercantile origins of the city – streets of butchers and brewers, of the herb market, of butter, pepper, herring and even meat and bread (Rue de Chair et Pain). Nowadays this is a vibrant city centre district of atmospheric bars and good restaurants, crowds and enticing little shops.

BRUSSELS: The City's Heart

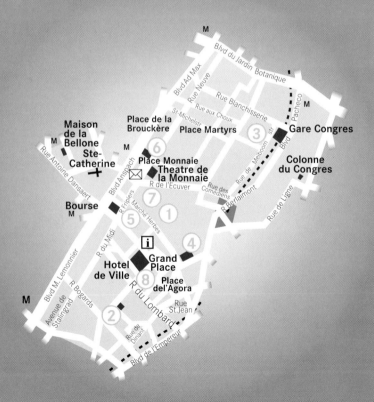

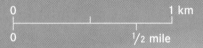

BEST OF

Brussels: The City's Heart

Getting there: **Metro:** The best metro stations for this area are Bourse/Beurs and De Brouckère. **Trams:** Tramlines 23, 52, 55, 56 and 81 pass through the district. **Train:** Gare Centrale/Centraal Station is a few minutes' walk away from Grand-Place.

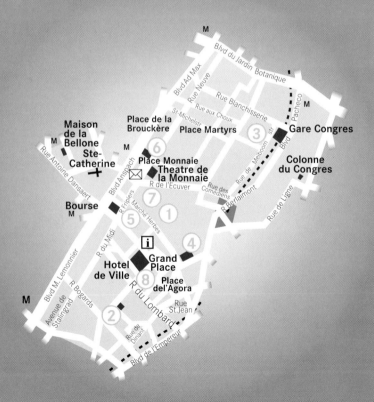

① L'Ilôt Sacré

The 'Sacred Little Island' – also known as 'The Belly of Brussels' – is the colourful nickname given to the very oldest streets close to Grand-Place, especially just east and north of the great square. Often dismissed as a mere tourist trap, it's one of the most picturesque and atmospheric parts of the city, as well as an excellent place to find a meal. **Pages 42–43**

② Mannekin Pis

What's the charm of this tasteless little guy? Top of many visitors' Must See list, the tiny metal-sculptured chap with the permanently full bladder turns out to be an endearing symbol of the city's political independence. **Pages 40–41**

③ Learn to like Tintin

Another child star of Belgian culture, Tintin, whose comic book series has sold in millions, is honoured in the fascinating Centre Belge de la Bande Dessinée (Belgian Cartoon-Strip Museum). This is also one of the best examples of Brussels' Art Nouveau architecture. **Pages 52–53**

④ Shop for chocs

Along with a multitude of other foodie stores, this neighbourhood has excellent chocolatiers with window displays like jewel-boxes. At some, you can sit and nosh on the premises. Some even give free samples. Try Neuhaus, in Galeries St-Hubert, they're one of the biggest names in Belgian chocolate, and invented the praline. **Pages 43, 51**

⑤ Go to church

This historic part of Brussels has about a dozen grandiose churches in a small area. Mainly in the gaudily decorative Flemish-Renaissance style, they make incongruous, dazzling oases of art and history amidst the touristy shops and bars. One of the most striking, though, is rather darker and moodier, the Eglise St-Nicholas in Rue au Beurre. It's the city's oldest church.

⑥ Get real

See the real Brussels in busy city squares that attract more locals, fewer tourists. Place de Brouckère and Place de la Monnaie are busy, modernised, commercial, while more run-down Place Ste-Cathérine is at the heart of a youthful, up-and-coming district. **Pages 46–47**

⑦ Chips with everything

To complete the Belgian experience, it's vital to wander the streets eating tasty french fries and mayonnaise from a pavement stall. It's the traditional local take away, and you'll see plenty in this area.

⑧ Get lucky

To head straight from Grand-Place to Mannekin Pis, leave the square by Rue Charles Buls. On the corner of Grand-Place and Rue Charles Buls, the golden figure on your left is of Everard t'Serclaes, who repulsed a 14th-century attack on the city. Locals used to believe that touching the statue brought good luck. Tourists still do.

Tourist information

Brussels' main tourist office is in Grand-Place, never more than a few minutes' walk from the sights in this area. There's also a regional tourist office, which includes Brussels information: *61 Rue du Marché aux Herbes. Tel: 504 0390.*

Mannekin Pis

In a more polite age, Mannekin was known as Petit Julien. With its chubby cheeks, petulant posture and boyish charm, the little statue is an imaginative and witty idea for a fountain. Instead of contriving the usual spouts of water emerging from fishes' mouths, seashells or other innocuous designs, sculptor Jérôme Duquesnoy depicted a small boy having a wee, an endless stream emerging from a tiny metal penis which he proudly points towards the viewer.

Standing on an unremarkable street corner, this tiny figure – it's under 60cm high – might have passed into obscurity, or might even have been removed by prudish city authorities. Somehow he captured the public imagination, and has found a permanent place in the city's consciousness. His prominence, however, has brought humiliation, and he has several times been stolen or vandalised, and was once even smashed to pieces.

Pissing through history

Duquesnoy's version was not the first. Brussels' pissing boy was originally carved from stone in the 15th century, a symbol of the Bruxellois spirit of defiance. In one legend, he extinguished the fuse of a bomb that threatened to blow up the Town Hall by weeing on it. Duquesnoy's bronze Mannekin appeared in 1619, looking rather spoiled and overfed, and was said to have been irreverently modelled on the son of Duke Gottfried of Lorraine.

His importance was such that Maximilian-Emmanuel of Bavaria (Governor of Brussels under King Charles II of Spain) presented the naked Mannekin with his first suit of clothes in 1698, by way of a suitably informal gesture of friendship towards the local people. In 1745, the boy was removed and vandalised by English troops (typical!) but when caught out they shamefacedly repaired and returned the miniature statue. French troops later made off with him. King Louis XV of France, in an effort to make amends, restored the statue to its proper place, presented him with the Cross of Louis XIV and gave him his second outfit, this time an exceptionally lavish brocade suit ornamented with gold thread.

Best-dressed poseur

From then on, despite his lack of domestic manners, the Mannekin's position in society was assured. Though naked much of the time, he has a bigger wardrobe than most of us. Numerous visiting heads of state and celebrities have donated clothes to the Mannekin and he now has over 600 different outfits (displayed at the **Brussels City Museum** in Grand-Place – *see page 29*). He even has his own official dressers – a man and a woman – who dress him every day at about 1000 and undress him at 1900.

His role as a symbol of the city has always made him a target for oddballs. In 1817, he was smashed to pieces by a local criminal, but the metal was recovered and recast in identical form. Political protestors, drunken revellers and vandals are drawn to inflict whatever indignities on him. Perhaps the greatest indignity is being cloned and mass-produced for souvenir shops. But still he survives, the eternal disrespectful toddler, eternally relieving himself without a care.

Getting there: Corner of Rue du Chêne and Rue de l'Etuve.

Ilôt Sacré

The heart and soul of old Brussels is here, hidden beneath the cobbles. The popular network of streets north and east of Grand-Place earned the name 'Sacred Isle' when environmental campaigners in the late 1950s used the name as a slogan to defend the area against the crass modern development that characterises other parts of the Belgian capital. The phrase succinctly summed up this historic quarter, a last link to the effervescent entrepreneurial spirit of the old Flemish Brussels. The campaign was successful and, instead of being knocked down, the area was handsomely restored in the 1960s.

Sacred Isle

Louis Quiévreux, the journalist who campaigned against modern urban development in the city centre, coined the name of the district, the Ilôt Sacré: 'We must protect an isle which is sacred!'

Many of the old houses are superb examples of Renaissance design, often with a traditional gable, stucco and tile or ceramic decoration on the façade. Thanks to the street performers, the wandering flower-sellers, the snack stalls and the multitude of eating places, the area, which is crammed with visitors, is full of life and energy. The street names themselves are like a feast, named after foods, herbs, spices and oils that were once sold at markets here, along with other wholesome and down-to-earth household goods. It is fun just to wander through these streets, some of which are pedestrianised, but don't miss the following highlights.

The **Rue de la Colline/Huevelstraat** leaves Grand-Place beside the Maison des Ducs de Brabant. At No 24, there's a glorious old house called La Balance; close by is an entrance into the Galeries Agora, a covered shopping area with inexpensive fashions.

The **Rue du Marché aux Herbes/Grasmarkt** is a bustling central street winding through the neighbourhood. At No 60 is the Belgian tourist office.

The **Rue des Bouchers/Beenhouwersstraat** is one of the most attractive and atmospheric of all the local streets, where restaurants lay out displays of game and fresh fish, tables are set up on both sides of the street and crowds flock to eat and listen to the buskers. Step into the side turn Impasse de la Fidelité to see the feminist answer to Mannekin Pis – the artless **Jannekin Pis**.

Just after, a turn on the right leads into **Petite Rue des Bouchers**, where the endearing little puppet theatre, **Théâtre de Toone**, lies up the Impasse Schuddeveld. Shows are in the local dialect, and there's an intriguing Puppet Museum on the premises, as well as a delightful café.

Rue du Marché aux Fromages/ Kaasmarkt is a lively late-night street. Here you'll see 'The Narrowest House in Brussels' – and it's quite a believable claim.

Galeries St-Hubert/Sint Hubertus Galerij is an elegant covered mall, nothing like modern malls. Over 150 years old, this was Europe's first mall, and it consists of real boutiques and shops along genuine streets and lanes (the *galeries*) enclosed within an impressive glass and cast-iron structure. Stroll under the glass arcades, window-shop and pause to be waited on at an 'outdoor' café table. It's stylish, and the names of the three *galeries* say it all: Roi (King), Prince and Galerie de la Reine (Queen). The latter has high-quality shopping, expensive jewellers and the famous *chocolatier* Neuhaus, inventor of praline and purveyors of mouthwatering delicacies to the rich and famous.

Getting there: between Mannekin Pis and Place de la Monnaie.

La Ville Ancienne
(The Old Quarter)

Brussels used to be a riverside city, and would perhaps be even more visually pleasing today if the sagacious late 19th-century city councillors, in particular the burgomaster Jules Anspach, had not decided to pave over the river and put streets on top. Ironically, he justified the move as a way of making Brussels healthier and more attractive: the slow-moving River Senne had become polluted and was blamed for a cholera outbreak in 1866.

Removing the river totally transformed this oldest and most beautiful part of Brussels, which had been similar in appearance to Bruges. It was replaced by modern squares and boulevards, one of which, of course, was named after the project's mastermind, Jules Anspach.

Yet that city-centre sense of history could not be eradicated. This was, after all, the original Brussels, where the first fortress had been constructed 1000 years ago on an island in the river, the Ile St-Géry, in the marshy place (*broek sella*) that gave the city its name. Though in need of a facelift, it remains a vital, thriving district, fashionable, feisty and upcoming, better known to locals than tourists. It's an arty, young, late-night area with a touch of sleaze, though known also for new fashion designers, clubs and discos, and authentic Bruxellois bars and restaurants.

Rue du Marché aux Charbon/Kolenmarkt, leading west and south out of Grand-Place, is a vibrant, upbeat street of entertainment and youthful crowds, with some good bars. Just a few paces north of it lies the similar **Place de la Bourse/Beursplein**, alongside Belgium's relatively sedate Stock Exchange, a neo-classical building with Rodin statues on the top.

Cross Boulevard Anspach to reach **Place St-Géry/Sint-Goriksplein**, where the beautiful 19th-century Halles (covered market-place) has been given a Covent-Garden-style restoration, turning it into an unusual and attractive shopping mall of glass, arches, balconies and wrought-ironwork. It stands on the Ile St-Géry, site of the original fortress around which the city first grew.

From the St-Géry market, take Pont de la Carpe – once a bridge over the River Senne – to the junction of Rue Antoine Dansaert, Rue Orts and Rue des Poissoniers. This is in the heart of an area due for restoration, where several young designers and artists have based themselves.

Place Ste-Cathérine, dominated by its 19th-century church, covers historic riverside quays, and some fine Flemish-Renaissance façades and gables survive. North of the square, the watery basin between Quai aux Briques and Quai aux Bois à Brûler used to be a river port. Quai aux Briques still has its important **Marché aux Poissons/Vismarkt** (Fish Market). Fishing boats no longer tie up here, but fish shops and restaurants still line the quayside.

Getting there: from Grand-Place to Ste-Cathérine.
Metro: Bourse.

Tunnel vision

Several of Brussels' metro stations have gigantic modern murals, some of them reminiscent of comic-strip style. Specially commissioned by the transport authority, these are all by distinguished Belgian artists. The tram passengers on the wall at the Bourse/Beurs station are by Paul Delvaux, the leading Surrealist. Other 'underground artists' used different media – at Comte de Flandres/ Graaf van Vlaanderen station, west of the Ville Ancienne area, 16 bronze figures by Paul van Hoeydonck enter the tunnel. Stokkel station has the inevitable Tintin.

Place de Brouckère/ De Brouckereplein

The city fathers' recurring dream of a modernised Brussels, free of its medieval inheritance, almost comes to pass in this so-called mini-Manhattan district, especially since the construction of such ugly shopping precincts as the Anspach Centre and (a few streets north) City 2. Yet this is a slice of the real, everyday Brussels and there remains a great deal worth seeing.

The streets north and west from De Brouckère have become squalid in parts, with tacky shopping along Rue Neuve and sleaze and sex along Rue de Laeken. Yet on the other side of Rue de Laeken is the church of **St-Jean Baptiste au Beguinage** (*Place du Beguinage/Begijnhof; open 0900–1700 (opens at 1000 on Tue); closed Sun, Mon, open some Sats; Free*). This is considered Belgium's best example of the Flemish-Baroque style, and all that remains of the large *beguinage* (a sort of lay monastery) that occupied much of this area in the Middle Ages.

Still a major highlight is the Belle Époque splendour of the **Metropole Hotel**, in Place de Brouckère, arguably the best hotel in the city. It's a reminder that this was once a *very* classy neighbourhood. If you're not staying there, at least take a seat in the amazing Metropole Café. Linger over a drink, listen to the pianist, gaze at the glass and stucco décor and ponder the lifestyle of pre-war aristocracy who regularly frequented this place.

In adjacent Place de la Monnaie/Munt much damage has been done by the looming **Anspach Centre**, the downmarket mall, which is, however, a useful shopping resource.

The square's gem is **Théâtre de la Monnaie/ Muntschouwburg** (*entrance in Rue Léopold; tel: 229 1211; box office open 1100–1730; tours of the building every Sat at noon, in French and Flemish only*), Brussels' world-class

> *Amour sacré de la patrie*
> *Rends-nous l'audace et la fierté!*
> *A mon pays je dois la vie,*
> *Il me devra la Liberté!*
>
> Sacred love of one's country
> Give us our courage and pride!
> To my country I owe life,
> To me it owes Liberty!

The song (by Scribe and Delavigne) that inspired the bourgeois Théâtre de la Monnaie audience to join protesting workers in the street at the start of the 1830 Revolution

opera house and home to Rosas, Anne Teresa de Keersmaeker's acclaimed modern dance company.

First built in 1697, reconstructed in 1819, and successfully enlarged in 1985, the opera house is one the city's proudest possessions. Behind an unremarkable neo-classical façade, the building preserves its grand 1819 décor.

It is said that the patriotic words of a song from *The Mute Girl of Portici* so touched opera-goers' hearts at a performance held here on 25 August 1830 that they leapt from their seats and went to join the workers outside who were protesting against foreign rule. That was the start of the 1830 Revolution which brought the Belgian state into being.

The martyrs of that revolution are honoured by scruffy **Place des Martyrs**, a few paces from Place de la Monnaie. Though run-down and neglected, the square is dominated by the monument in their memory.

Getting there: 500m north of Grand-Place.
Metro: De Brouckère. Bus: 29, 60, 65, 66, 71.

Eating and Drinking

Every day after work, and all day at weekends, locals pour into this central quarter from all over the city for a good meal, a drink or a night out. There's a huge range of bars, cafés and restaurants, covering all budgets and including places of great style and history, as well as plain and simple outlets suitable for an inexpensive meal or snack. Wander in any direction from Grand-Place to find dozens of equally tempting places.

Cafés and bars

L'Archiduc

6 Rue Antoine Dansaert. Tel: 512 0652. Open 1600 till about 0500 daily. ££. Authentic 1930s décor, often a little bit of gentle live music, relaxed comfortable mood, popular for chilling out at the end of the night.

Le Cirio

18–20 Rue de la Bourse. Tel: 512 1395. Open 1000–0100 daily. £££. For a high-priced drink in fabulous *fin-de-siècle* splendour, this is the place. It was the originator of *half-en-half* (mixed champagne and white wine), and that's still the drink to order here.

Le Falstaff

19–25 Rue Henri Maus. Tel: 511 9877. Opens 2230 nightly, closes around 0300 weekdays, 0500 weekends. ££. Spacious, arranged in several rooms, popular day and night with every kind of local and tourist, this brasserie alongside the Bourse is a model of Art Nouveau décor. Its huge terrace is a particular draw (even in winter, when it is heated).

Café Metropole

31 Place de Brouckère. Tel: 219 2384. Open 0900–0100 daily. £££. Located inside the Metropole Hotel, famous for its extravagant *fin-de-siècle décor*, high ceilings, gleaming mirrors and stucco, this place is a Brussels institution. Snacks, pastries, teas, as well as drinks.

A La Mort Subite

7 Rue Montagne aux Herbes Potagères. Tel: 512 8664. Opens around 1030 Mon–Fri, 1100 Sat, 1230 Sun, closes around 0100. ££. The name's meaning, 'Sudden Death', might seem off-putting, but this old brasserie is a picture-perfect traditional Brussels bar, busy, atmospheric, and specialising in its own beer – the eponymous Mort Subite.

Restaurants

L'Achepot

1 Place Ste-Cathérine. Tel: 511 6221. Lunch and dinner, closed Sun. £–££. Appealing, popular restaurant, in the former river-harbour area, with informal and relaxed atmosphere. Traditional local dishes, especially sweetbreads and offal (brains, kidneys etc), are well prepared and served at moderate prices.

L'Alban Chambon

31 Place de Brouckère. Tel: 217 7650. Lunch and dinner daily. £££. The restaurant of the classy Metropole Hotel offers top-class French cuisine in a luxurious, if pricey, setting.

Aux Armes de Bruxelles

13 Rue des Bouchers. Tel: 511 2118. Open Tue–Sun 1200–2315. ££. In contrast to the touristy eateries round about, this smart, crisp, relatively upmarket fish restaurant has great local atmosphere, good service and well-prepared international favourites, as well as local specialities, such as *waterzooi* (fish stew) and mussels.

La Belle Maraîchère

11 Place Ste-Cathérine. Tel: 512 9759. Lunch and dinner, closed Wed, Thur. ££. One of the best, and best-known, of the smart little fish restaurants on the former river quayside at Ste-Cathérine's. It's good value, and specialises in traditional Flemish dishes, such as *waterzooi*, a stew made with three kinds of fish.

Chez Leon

18 Rue des Bouchers. Tel: 511 1415. Open 1200–2300 daily. ££. The classic example of a popular 'Brussels mussels' eatery, where huge amounts of this local favourite dish are well prepared and briskly served with tasty chips in a busy, no-nonsense ambience.

Comme Chez Soi

23 Place Rouppe. Tel: 512 2921. Lunch and dinner, closed Sun, Mon, 25 Dec–1 Jan, and all July. £££. The name means 'Like Home', but few homes resemble this Belle Epoque grandeur in an Art Nouveau setting. Here Belgium's King of Chefs, the famous Pierre Wynants, uses traditional Flemish recipes and ingredients – beer and offal, for example – as well as ideas and ingredients from the French and German regions of the country to create an exceptional Belgian *haute cuisine*. Specialities include *filets de sole* with Riesling, and prawn *mousseline*. French and Belgian gourmets fill the place nightly, so book ahead.

Martens

28 Rue Antoine Dansaert. Tel: 511 0631. Lunch and dinner, closed Sun, Mon. ££. Much liked by the trendy young locals of the Rue Dansaert for its fresh, modern French cuisine, this restaurant – typical of the area – has austere bare-brick décor, high ceilings and reasonable prices.

L'Ogenblick

1 Galerie des Princes. Tel: 511 6151. Lunch and dinner, closed Sun. ££–£££. Relaxed and informal but pricey Galeries St-Hubert restaurant in a beautifully preserved traditional Brussels bar.

49

Les Quatre Saisons

2 Rue de l'Homme Chrétien. Tel: 505 5100. Lunch and dinner, closed Sat lunch and 20 July–17 Aug. £££. A few paces southeast from Grand-Place. Rich and creamy French cuisine at one of the city's most upmarket restaurants, located in the Hotel Royal Windsor.

Taverne du Passage

30 Galerie de la Reine. Tel: 512 3731. Open 1200–2400 daily. £–££. One of the highlights of the Galeries Saint-Hubert arcades, this traditional 70-year-old brasserie serves good snacks and meals of classic Belgian specialities, such as *choucroute au jambonneau* (ham and pickled cabbage).

Vincent

8–10 Rue des Dominicains. Tel: 502 3693. Warm, atmospheric old tiled brasserie in a side street off Rue des Bouchers, specialising in Belgian classics, such as *carbonnade* (beer and beef stew) and pots of mussels.

Tip

Brussels is a late, late city. Don't turn up at clubs and discos before midnight. Most clubs open at 2300, but don't hot up until 0100. The usual plan is meet up with friends in a bar until midnight, then make your way to one of the many clubs. Leave at dawn and return to a bar for an early breakfast. By the way, regardless of whether the club has an entry charge you must usually tip the doorman at least 50BEF (that's after he's decided to let you in).

Clubs and nightlife

L'Acrobat

*14–16 Rue Borgval.
Open 2100–0400 Fri and Sat only. Free.* Effective mix of styles, of people and of age-groups.

Cercle 52

52 Rue des Chartreux. Open 2200–0600 Thur–Sun. Entrance fee. Anything goes gay venue with thumping music and dark rooms.

Espace de Nuit

*10 Rue Marché aux Fromages.
Open 2200–0600 daily. Free.* Touristy but good disco on several floors of this old building in the heart of the historic quarter.

Who's Whose Land

17 Rue Poinçon. Open 2100–0300 Fri, Sat and Sun. Entrance fee. Highly rated, very fashionable late-night disco. Sunday night is gay.

Shopping

Around Grand-Place is the city's major shopping area, especially for specialist gourmet food and drink. The lanes of the 'Ilôt Sacré' have interesting, but touristy, stores, while for a classier, more authentic range stroll in the historic glass-covered Galeries St-Hubert.

Here wealthy Bruxellois window-shop, take tea, and buy jewellery and fashion accessories. It's strong on *chocolatiers*, including Neuhaus, inventor of the praline and still considered one of the very best.

Place Ste-Cathérine was a fishing harbour before the River Senne was covered over, and remains the preserve of fish merchants as well as connoisseur foodie stores, such as the excellent Ferme Landaise.

Rue du Midi, unexpectedly, is devoted to philatelists and numismatists, with serious-minded stamp collectors who come here from all over the world.

Rue Antoine Dansaert is the heart of a young, chic area where several new designers have shops.

Rue Neuve is the locals' main shopping street. Heading north from the Brouckère/Monnaie squares, it connects two popular shopping malls, the Anspach Centre and City 2. Here mid-range chains, including Bennetton and Marks & Spencer, rub shoulders with budget outlets.

www.belgianfries.com

Yes, there's a whole website devoted solely to the subject of Belgian 'French fries', known on the site, naturally, as Belgian Fries. As well as explaining just why Belgian *fries are so delicious, and exactly how to make them, it reveals that* French *fries are much thinner and greasier. If you want a taste of real, not virtual fries, there are open-air stalls in many of the squares. Eat them with mayonnaise.*

Cartoon-Strip Brussels

Over 200 million Tintin books have now been sold, in 51 languages. Thundering Typhoons!

Trading on Tintin's amazing worldwide success the city of Brussels decided to make cartoons a local speciality and likes to call itself Europe's cartoon-strip capital. This is an exaggeration – other cities could claim the title (Dundee, home to several thriving children's comics, springs to mind). In truth, the rather creepy kid with the quiff, together with his talking dog Snowy (Milou in the original), the whisky-soaked reprobate Captain Haddock and all the other Tintin characters are the only really successful Belgian cartoon creation.

However, several other cartoonists were Belgian (mainly French-speaking), and comic connoisseurs sometimes speak of a 'Belgian school' of cartoon drawing. Tintin's author, **Hergé** (real name Georges Rémi, 1907–83), devised other comic-book series, notably *Quick* and *Flupke*, but these achieved little success compared to the fame of the 'boy reporter', who first appeared in 1929. For popularity, Tintin's runner-up would be Morris's Lucky Luke, mainly known in the French-speaking world, where he is pronounced as 'Lookie Look'. Other Belgian cartoon successes, mostly bigger hits with francophones than English-speakers, include *The Smurfs* (by Peyo), *Spirou* (by Rob-Vel), *Gaston Lagaffe* (by André Franquin) and *Blake and Morrison* (Edgar Pierre Jacobs).

La Centre Belge de la Bande Dessinée (The Belgian Cartoon-Strip Centre)

La Centre Belge de la Bande Dessinée, 20 Rue des Sables/Zandstraat. Tel: 219 1980. Open Tue–Sun 1000–1800. Closed Mon and some national holidays. Train station: Congress. Bus: 38, 58, 61. Trams: 90, 92, 93, 94. Admission: £££.

The Centre honours Belgium's clutch of comic-book authors on several floors. It is one of the city's most unusual attractions. Its most interesting and entertaining section explains how comics are drawn and printed. A small cinema shows videos on the subject, and you might come out liking Tintin a little more than when you went in.

Films are also shown on the Art Nouveau style, and for many visitors the most striking feature of the Cartoon-Strip Centre is that it occupies one of the finest Art Nouveau buildings in Brussels (or the world). This is one of **Victor Horta's** masterpieces, originally built in 1906 as a warehouse (*see page 87*).

The comic-strip trail

Thanks to the popularity of Belgian comic strips, the city has commissioned half a dozen dramatic, surprising and amusing cartoon murals painted on gable ends around the city centre. A map showing their locations is available from the tourist office.

Brussels: The Royal Quarter

Palatial buildings, important museums, grand avenues and white mansions in proud Classical style, stand on the Coudenburg slope rising southeast of the city's historic core. When the French nobility moved into Brussels at the end of the 18th century, they created this dignified 'Upper Town' on the site that had already served as the home of the Dukes of Burgundy.

BRUSSELS: The Royal Quarter

BEST OF

Brussels:
The Royal Quarter

Getting there: **Metro:** *The nearest Metro station to most of the area is Porte de Namur. Metro station Parc/Park is better for the Cathedral and the northern part of the area.*
Trams: *Tramlines 92, 93 and 94 run along Rue Royale (Koningsstraat) and the Rue de la Régence (Regentschapsstraat) through the middle of the area.*
Buses: *38, 60 and 71 run through the area.*
Train: *Gare Centrale/Centraal Station and Gare Chappelle/Kapel are both a few minutes' walk from all the sights of the Royal Quarter.*

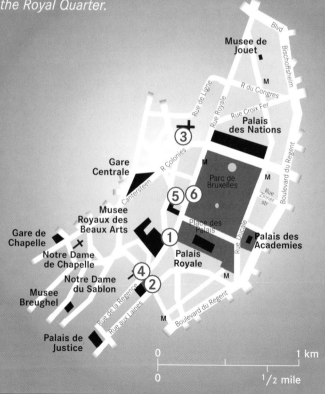

① Place Royale

Just take in the inspiring sweep of this majestic pale neo-Classical square, one of the loveliest sights in the city. It still retains a stately harmony of style. From the statue in the centre of the square, there's an excellent view of the Town Hall tower in Grand-Place. **Pages 58–59**

② Musical Instrument Museum

In 1999 the wonderful Musical Instrument Museum is scheduled to move into the strange, dark, wrought-iron setting of the magnificent Art Nouveau former Old England department store. **Page 59**

③ Go to church

A magnificent piece of Gothic style, the city's cathedral has recently been fully restored. It's packed with artistic treasures, especially the stained glass on the west side. **Pages 60–61**

④ The Sablon Squares

The twin squares of Grand and Petit Sablon (Zavel in Flemish) at the southern edge of the area are a smart enclave of antique dealers, luxury stores and famous restaurants – including the one where President Clinton went to dinner during his Brussels visit. Have tea at Wittamer's. **Pages 62–63**

⑤ Flemish Masters

Discover the great Medieval and Renaissance art of Flanders on the Blue Tour at the Royal Museum of Ancient Art, with its famous works by van der Weyden, Memling, Bruegel and collections of Flemish Primitives. **Pages 64–65**

⑥ Get Surreal

Both the Modern and Ancient section of the Royal Museums of Art give insights into the development of Belgian Surrealism, and show some of the best-known of the amazing images created by Ensor and the rival leaders of the movement, Magritte and Delvaux. **Pages 64–65**

When to come

Monday is not a good day. The Royal Museums of Art and other museums, and even the church in Place Royale, are all closed.

Belle Époque

As Rue Royale passes beyond Parc de Bruxelles and leaves the Royal Quarter, it passes some good examples of Belle Époque architecture, its elegance now looking a little out of place. Pause at Hotel Astoria, 101–103 Rue Royale. Built for the 1910 World Fair, it was once a favourite of the super-rich. Guests included the Aga Khan, whose wife used to ask for her bath to be filled with asses' milk – supposedly good for the skin.

Place Royale/ Koningsplein

Place Royale, Rue Royale and Palais Royal/Koningsplein, Koningstraat and Koninglijk Paleis. Trams 92, 93 and 94 run along Rue Royale (Koningsstraat) to Place Royale and the Palais Royal. Buses 38, 60 and 71 also run through the area.

Brussels is a city of perspectives, of grand urban landscapes. That's especially so here on the Coudenberg hill rising east of the historic centre. Glimpses of the Lower Town are interspersed with the inspiring sweep of terraces and avenues created by leading French architects of the late 18th century.

The focal point is the **Royal Square**, a beautiful Classical composition, perfectly symmetrical, with exquisite creamy white mansions. In the centre stands the triumphalist statue of Godefroid de Bouillon, the Norman 'King of Jerusalem' following the First Crusade. The **Church of St Jacques sur Coudenberg** (*open Tue–Sat 1000–1800, Mon 1500–1800*) stands alongside the square, while adjacent to it is the Royal Palace.

The Royal Palace

Open in summer only (usually approx 21 July–21 Sept), 0930–1530. Closed Mon. Free.

Originally the palace of the Dukes of Burgundy, this Brussels residence was a by-word throughout Western Europe for luxury. Together with much else in the Dukes' Coudenberg estate, it was destroyed in February 1731 by a huge fire, supposedly started in the palace kitchen. On these fire-damaged ruins the new French palace was constructed in the 1770s. Today, excavations are uncovering fascinating remnants of the Ducal Palac, in particular part of its lovely paved floors.

The Royal Palace is not – and never has been – the home of any monarch, though it does serve as a ceremonial residence for the Belgian King and Queen on state occasions. The palace is open to the public only in summer, and only when the king is not present. Though a little austere in atmosphere, the palace entrance, great staircase, throne room and immense great antechamber are extremely rich in décor and design.

Rue Royale

Alongside the square on one side rises the **Royal Arts Museums** (*see pages 64–65*) in what used to be the palace of Charles of Lorraine; on the other side, 2km-long Rue Royale extends majestically into the distance alongside the royal park, **Parc de Bruxelles/Park van Brussel**. At No 13, notice the slightly out-of-place Art Nouveau shopfront – a perfect example of the style. North of the Parc, the road looks less royal, finally becoming unappealing and threatening at its northern end.

Musée des Instruments de Musique/ Muziekinstrumentenmuseum

'Old England', Rue Villa Hermosa. Moving from 17 Petit Sablon. Tel: 512 0848 or 511 3595. New opening details not arranged. Entrance charge not arranged.

A few Art Nouveau gems intrude into the neo-Classical harmony of the area. The most spectacular is the dark wrought-iron and glass landmark that used to be the Old England department store. Standing just off the Royal Square, this 1899 masterpiece was scheduled to be demolished by order of the city council. Protesters won a stay of execution, and at last even the council could see the value of restoring it. This work was due to be completed by the end of 1999, and Brussels' large Museum of Musical Instruments has found a home here. Exhibits range from 17th-century wind instruments to tiny Victorian household pianos, from bagpipes made of a whole animal to a genuine former violin-maker's workshop. One important room is devoted to **Adolphe Sax**, innovative Belgian brass instrument maker and creator of the saxophone. In the children's room, the very young can experiment with sound and music.

Domes

In 1902, King Léopold asked architect Henri Maquet to redesign the frontage of the Royal Palace. Unfortunately, the king was not entirely happy with the result. In particular, he didn't like the new domes on top of the pavilions at each end of the curved galleries. Determined not to use the architect again, King Léopold used to refer to the domes as 'The covers of Monsieur Maquet's coffin'.

The Cathedral and Park

North of Place Royale and the Palais. Metro: Parc/Park. Trams 92, 93 and 94. Buses 38, 60 and 71.

The Cathedral of Saints Michael and Gudule

Place Ste-Gudule. Tel: 217 8345. Open Apr–Oct 0700–1900 Mon–Fri, 0730–1900 Sat, 0800–1900 Sun. Rest of year – closes an hour earlier. Admission to crypt: £.

This beautiful pale building, outstanding example of Gothic art and workmanship, stands on the Treurenberg hill between the Coudenberg and the Lower Town. Despite the powerful, imposing position, it suffers from the planning errors of the municipal authorities, who permitted unsightly modern structures and busy roads to press against the cathedral on all sides.

The **twin towers** show the influence of French architects and builders, as this feature is almost unknown locally. Approached on the west side by a monumental staircase, the cathedral is a mass of delicate carving. Inside and out, the evolving Gothic styles, from the earliest to the latest, come together harmoniously. Once inside, turn and admire the deeply-coloured **stained glass** on the west side – perhaps the cathedral's most attractive feature. There's more good stained glass in the chancel, and don't miss the richly carved **pulpit** showing Adam and Eve being cast out of the Garden of Eden.

The cathedral is tainted by the subject matter of one of its greatest treasures, the stained glass above the altar of the **Chapelle du Saint-Sacrement**, to the left of the choir. Built in 1540, it attempts to justify the anti-semitic outrage 140 years earlier in which four local Jewish families were slaughtered. It does, though, give an insight into the perverse piety of the attackers, who claimed that the sacramental wafers had been stolen by Jews on Good Friday and ritually stabbed, the miracle being that blood spurted from the biscuits – the so-called Miracle of the Holy Sacraments. Such accusations and murders were common throughout Europe.

Damaged during the French bombardment which destroyed Grand-Place, the building has seen many repairs, additions

and changes over the centuries. Originally built in the 15th century on the site of an earlier church, Brussels' cathedral was dedicated to the male and female patron saints of the city. In Rome, the papal officials were asking – 'who is Gudule'? Michael refers to the Archangel Michael, but **Gudule**, it emerged, was a pious local Flemish woman who had never been beatified. The cathedral was requested to remove her name from its title, and readily agreed to do so. For all that, it has been known as Saints Michael and Gudule ever since. To give her further honour, the square outside is also called Gudule.

Parc de Bruxelles

Rue Royale starts near the cathedral, and runs in a majestic 2km sweep alongside Parc de Bruxelles to Place Royale. The Parc is the only disappointment in the superb array of regal splendour here. Though still enclosed by its palatial buildings, the formal park, created by Hapsburg Empress Maria Theresa, has become a dull, unremarkable spot for a picnic or a rest. Before the 1731 fire, these grounds were for the exclusive use of the ruling family, who could hunt stag or boar here, and enjoy jousting.

" *Numbers of statues decorate the place, the very worst I ever saw. These cupids must have been erected in the time of the Dutch dynasty, as I judge from the immense posterior developments.* "

William Thackeray, writing about the Parc de Bruxelles, 1815

Le Sablon/Zavel

In and around Place du Grand Sablon and Place du Petit Sablon/Grote Zavel and Kleine Zavel. Trams: 92, 93 and 94. Buses: 20 and 48.

In both languages, the name means a place of sand, for swampy quicksands once lay here south of the Ducal Palace. There's no sand now, and the waters were drained away centuries ago. Instead, the two fine squares of Grand and Petit Sablon, connected by the Sablon/Zavel church, make a smart little district long ago favoured by the aristocracy. It's a classy, stylish, sometimes slightly stuffy but thoroughly charming enclave of restored 17th and 18th-century townhouses, antiques emporia, luxury stores, chic tearooms and famous restaurants.

Grand Sablon/Grote Zavel, the larger of the two squares, is an agreeable place to linger over a coffee and cake, especially at Café Wittamer, famous not just for pastries but for film-star clientele. Across the road is top Brussels *chocolatier* Pierre Marcolini. The square is still among the most sought-after addresses in Brussels, though nothing like the days when Europe's leading aristocratic families had homes here. Even at that time, weekly markets were held in the square, and every weekend there is a street market, partly under canvas, where connoisseurs can tell the antiques from the bric-à-brac.

Cobbled little **Rue de Rollebeek** descends steeply from this upscale neighbourhood to the run-down historic working-class area called Marolles (*see page 74*). Lined with outdoor tables and restaurants and antique stores, it makes its way down to the Gothic church of **Notre-Dame de la Chapelle/Kapellekerk**, where the Flemish master Pieter Bruegel the Elder is buried (*see page 74 for Marolles*).

Eglise Notre-Dame-du-Sablon

The Sablon district started with the building of a church up here by the Guild of Crossbowmen in 1304. Pilgrims came to see its miraculous statue of the Virgin Mary, endowments and donations were gathered, and the church became wealthy. The Crossbowmen decided to enlarge and redesign their church, and the result was a **Flamboyant Gothic masterpiece** with fine stained glass and stone carvings. Take a look at the pulpit, a feast of baroque imagery. The exterior of the church was again reworked in the 19th century, adding yet more exuberant decoration. The church's 'miraculous' statue used to be carried in triumph at the head of the annual Ommegang procession which starts from here and makes its way to the Grand-Place.

Petit Sablon/Kleine Zavel

For the Musical Instrument Museum, 17 Petit Sablon, see page 59.

For the Musical Instrument Museum, 17 Petit Sablon, see page 59.

The present square was laid out just over 100 years ago, and most houses date from that time, though the King of Spain's House is much older. **Karl Marx** lived here in 1845, before the square took on its present shape. It's a pretty space with a lovely Renaissance garden behind elaborate wrought-iron gates. Here 48 bronze **statues** – in fact only 47 since one was stolen – depict the ancient crafts of the city. It's hard now to work out what they are: the art of the tallowmaker, for example, is represented by a bottle and a dead goose. Also in the gardens, statues stand in memory of Count Egmont and Count Horne, who tried to have the Inquisition abolished, struggled against Spanish domination of the Low Countries, and eventually were beheaded for their trouble. The grandiose **Palais d'Egmont**, on one side of the square, now belonging to the Belgian Foreign Ministry, is where the treaty was signed in 1972 admitting the UK and Ireland into the European Common Market.

Pilgrims

The Guild of Crossbowmen set up the city's first police force, even though the fame and fortune of their Sablon church started with a shady legend and an unsolved crime. Eager to attract pilgrims, the Guild installed a statue of the Virgin Mary – supposedly with miraculous powers – which had been stolen from a church in Antwerp. It was not clear who was responsible for the theft, but the plan worked, and the pilgrims came.

Royal Museums of Fine Art

3 Rue de la Régence. 508 3211. Open Tue–Sun; Modern Art 1000–1300, 1400–1700; Ancient Art 1000–1200, 1300–1700. Free. Metro: Centrale or Parc. Tram: 92, 93 and 94.

Rising imposingly from Place Royale (the entrance is in Rue de la Régence), the **Museum of Ancient Art** is housed in a grim, formal palace founded by Napoleon for the overflow from the Louvre in Paris. It soon became one of Europe's leading art museums in its own right, with particular emphasis on the great works of Flanders. In 1984, the **Museum of Modern Art** was added, its eight storeys almost entirely underground. The two together cover more than 600 years of fine art.

Musée d'Art Ancien/Museum van Oude Kunst

Three different marked routes guide visitors around the highlights of the vast collection in the Museum of Ancient Art. The **Blue Tour** (15th–16th centuries) takes in some of the most valuable and outstanding of the works displayed, including Rogier van der Weyden, Hans Memling and his followers, Hieronymus Bosch, Pieter Bruegel the Elder and Pieter Brueghel the Younger, and the other Flemish Primitives. The subject matter is almost always religious, until the appearance of landscapes at the end of the period. The **Brown Tour** (17th–18th centuries) looks at many remarkable works from this period, but the collection is overwhelmingly dominated by Rubens.

The **Yellow Tour** (19th century) shows vividly the clashing styles of the century, with neo-Classical and Romantic works at the start and Impressionists, neo-Impressionists and a Belgian school called Luminists at the finish. Don't miss Room 88, with its superb collection, including Gauguin, Bonnard, Seurat and Signac. Interesting too are the strange works by James Ensor, considered to be at the start of Surrealism.

Musée d'Art Moderne/ Museum van Moderne Kunst

Can be entered via 3 Rue de la Régence, but also has its own entrance at 1 Place Royale.

All the major strands of modern art are well represented in this spacious, light, airy underground building. There are sections devoted to Fauvism, Expressionism, Cubism, Abstract Art, the various Sixties movements and contemporary schools of today. There are several works by members of the radical COBRA group (the name is short for Copenhagen, Brussels and Amsterdam) of the 1940s, 1950s and 1960s, whose art was characterised by total freedom of expression. Most of the leading Belgian exponents of all these movements are here, as well as some outstanding foreign works, including paintings by Picasso, Chagall and Dali.

The most important area in the museum is **Surrealism**, on Levels 5 and 6, which retrospectively includes several artists who did not consider themselves part of the movement, notably Paul Delvaux. He, together with fellow Bruxellois René Magritte, were in the front rank of Surrealism. The **Magritte Room** on Level 6 contains 26 of the artist's paintings, including some of the most familiar and striking. Many less well-known Belgian Surrealists have a place in the museum, as do other leading artists in the field, including Man Ray, Salvador Dali, Max Ernst, Joan Miró and the Italian, de Chirico, who influenced Magritte to take up Surrealism.

Cafés and Bars

Place du Grand Sablon

Many good cafés and brasseries cling to the edges of the Grand Sablon square. The outdoor tables of one mingle with those of its neighbour, and anyway there's not much to tell them apart. The daytime patrons are a show-off mix of tourists, locals and antique hunters. In the evening, some of the bars stay open very late and cater to a younger clientele.

Rue des Minimes

Leading off Place du Grand Sablon, this street has a different character and bars like Café Richard or Pitt's Bar (pronounced Pete's) open early and close very late (sometimes 0500). During the day, they make a smart spot for drinks or lunch, but come alive with loud music and a younger crowd in the evening.

Wittamer

12–13 Place du Grand Sablon. Tel: 512 3742. Open Mon 0800–1800, Tue–Sat 0700–1900, Sun 0700–1800. £££. This is *the* Sablon tearooms, ultra chic and pricey, where you can sit indoors or outside at chrome tables under plain canvas parasols watching the world over excellent sorbets, pastries and coffees.

De Ultieme Hallucinatie

316 Rue Royale. Tel: 217 0614. Open 1100–0200 daily. £££. There's a frenzy of authentic iron, wood and glass Art Nouveau décor inside this highly rated but inconspicuous bar-restaurant at the wrong end of Rue Royale. A wide choice of beers, and excellent but expensive meals available at lunch and dinner times – try fish poached in *geuze* beer.

Restaurants

Lola

33 Place du Grand Sablon. Tel: 514 2460. Lunch and dinner daily. ££. Imaginative French cooking, such as rabbit with orange blossom, plus some veggie options, in a place popular with Sablon locals.

Aux Bons Enfants

49 Place du Grand Sablon. Tel: 512 4095. Lunch and dinner daily exc Wed. £. Simple down-to-earth eatery with wooden beams and basic, popular cooking. Among the lowest prices in the area.

L'Ecailler du Palais Royale

18 Rue Boedenbroeck. Tel: 512 8751. Lunch and dinner daily exc Sun. £££. Super-posh Sablon restaurant with the best of everything for a thoroughly respectable class of diner. First-class classic French cooking, specialising in fish and seafood – one of the best in Belgium.

Shopping

Antiques

In addition to the big weekend antiques market in Place du Grand Sablon, the square and its surrounding streets has several antique shops where the discerning may find a good piece, and perhaps at a good price. Look in Rue de la Paille, Rue des Minimes, Rue de Rollebeek.

Chocolate shops

Chocolatier Mary

73 Rue Royale. Acclaimed for excellent pralines and other gourmet chocolates.

Pierre Marcolini

39 Place du Grand Sablon. Tel: 514 1206. Considered by many to be the best of Belgium's *chocolatiers*, and winner of international awards for patisserie, this civilised shop is a feast of sight and scent as well as taste, with its beautiful chocolates and little cakes. Many are encrusted with genuine gold (to be eaten), and the whole display is more reminiscent of a jewellers. Wonderful – eat now or take home.

Wittamer

12–13 Place du Grand Sablon. Tel: 512 3742. The famed Sablon tearoom (*see page 66*) also sells delectable handmade chocs and other high-quality treats.

Nightlife

Some Sablon bars become discos after dark, and stay open very late, even all night. One of the most popular is **Pitt's** (*53 Rue des Minimes*).

What to try or buy

Don't shy away from 'tourist' places; they often have the very best of traditional products. Always make sure that lace and chocolates are authentically handmade and Belgian. Local people, by contrast, would be more likely to buy cheaper imported lace from the Far East and factory-made chocolates which are not up to the high standard of the classic handmade Belgian chocs.

Surreal Belgium

Something in the Belgian soul adores the bizarre, paradoxical and irreconcilable ... in short, the surreal. And they prefer it to be buttoned up with a constrained normality. René Magritte said the aim of Surrealist art was to find the marvellous within the ordinary.

He himself was the perfect example. A respectable married man living with his wife Georgette in a nicely furnished house in a Brussels suburb, **René Magritte** (1898–1967) deplored the Bohemianism affected by his fellow artists. Instead of using a studio, he preferred to paint at home, setting up the easel on his expensive drawing-room carpet.

His paintings likewise have a deceptive, disturbing air of the commonplace. In the street it's night-time, while in the sky above it is broad daylight, as in the *The Empire of Lights* – look more closely and find shadows of objects that aren't there. *The Rape* is a portrait of a woman – but the face is her naked body. In *The Black Magic* a naked woman stands on a stone balcony: half of her, coloured blue, seems unreal, perhaps marble, while the lower half is sensually alive. What does it mean? Typically, Magritte answered that his pictures had no meaning at all. Just like everything else.

Paul Delvaux (1897–1994), though more 'arty' than Magritte, also lived an irreproachable suburban life with his second wife Tam. His works depict a dreamy, fantastic world of the naked and the dead, where ordinary citizens mingle with nude figures, erotically half-clad women, skeletons.

The Expressionist **James Ensor** (1860–1949), who lived above his parents' souvenir shop in Ostend, painted odd, incomprehensible scenes said to lie at the beginnings of Surrealism. Yet the same tendency can be seen even in

> **❝** *Ceci n'est pas un pipe*
> ('This is not a pipe') **❞**

René Magritte's title for his picture of a pipe

medieval Belgian artists like Hieronymus Bosch (1450–1516), whose work is characterised by the bizarre in everyday life. A hundred years later, Pieter Brueghel's surreal *Fall of Icarus* depicts working men and animals not even bothering to look as the winged Icarus crashes down from heaven and disappears into the sea.

Leave the museums and look around: the surreal is everywhere in Brussels. Even the architecture – over-the-top Flemish Baroque, with its statuary climbing right out of the façades, or the wildly swirling, hallucinatory shapes of Art Nouveau – reflects the same cast of mind. Magritte used to find inspiration as he sat with a drink at **La Fleur en Papier Doré** in Rue des Alexiens or played chess at **Le Greenwich** in Rue des Chartreux. It is all too easy to imagine.

69

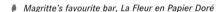

Magritte's favourite bar, La Fleur en Papier Doré

Brussels: Outer Districts

The ancient heart of Brussels is so compact that some of its most interesting areas and famous sights are only a short bus or tram (or taxi) ride away from the centre. For shops, bars, restaurants and entertainment, or to see Brussels icons such as the Atomium, it's worth exploring the city's outer districts.

71

BRUSSELS: Outer Districts

BEST OF

Brussels: Outer Districts

Getting there: Even to these suburban or off-centre locations, journey times are short. From Grand-Place to the far flung Atomium is just 6km. Everywhere is easily accessible by tram, bus or metro, or taxi if preferred. To use the public transport system, a ticket must be automatically stamped when it begins to be used, and is valid for an hour (or a single journey, if longer than an hour). It is cheaper to buy a carnet of 10 tickets. Access details are given for each page in this section.

① Art Nouveau

Few cities anywhere have as much surviving Art Nouveau architecture as Brussels, despite the best efforts of the city council to demolish it and modernise. The 'high priest' of this early-20th-century style was Victor Horta. His own home and others nearby are perfect examples.
Pages 86-87

② Atomium

In contrast to the endearing miniaturised sights like Mini-Europe and the Mannekin Pis, here's an iron molecule magnified 168 billion times! Constructed for the 1958 World Fair as a symbol of the scientific future, it now has a charmingly dated quality – and is one of Brussels' best-known attractions. **Page 80**

③ Mini-Europe

The capital cities of Europe are cut down to size (on a precise scale of 1 to 25) at this highly enjoyable must-see attraction in the Bruparck leisure area, close to the Atomium at Heysel. Other Bruparck features include an all-round cinema, a water park and several inexpensive eating places. **Pages 80-81**

④ Maxi-Europe

Brussels is probably best known, worldwide, as the 'capital of Europe' – slightly inaccurate since Luxembourg and Strasbourg share the role. The European quarter just east of the centre is where this awesome, rather autocratic power is based. Not a pretty sight, but an interesting one. **Pages 78-79**

⑤ Louise/Louiza

Many locals never get nearer to the city centre than this. Avenue Louise, Place Louise, and the surrounding avenues, streets and lanes are Brussels' busy, real-life main shopping district, with department stores, designer outlets, upmarket specialist shops, cafés and restaurants. **Page 75**

⑥ Les Marolles / Marollen

Just south of the city centre and tourist heartland lies this gritty traditional working-class neighbourhood. It's a historic district with plenty of character and its own patois mixing Flemish and French, though all of that is dying out as the area becomes better known as a centre of youthful, anything-goes entertainment. **Page 74**

73

South of the centre
Marolles/Marollen

Buses 20 (from the east) and 48 (from the Bourse) serve the Marolles.

This resolutely proletarian quarter lies south of the Grand-Place, and was always a home for the artisan class. With the paving-over of the River Senne, many of the skilled workers moved out and the area went downhill socially, attracting prostitutes. Part of the Marolles was destroyed with the building of the immense Palais de Justice law courts, which looms over the poor streets. In theory, it's a place of great working-class pride and tradition, and is the home of the strange Brussels dialect which mixes Flemish and French and is impenetrable to outsiders. In practice, you probably won't hear the patois, and Marolles has become a district where immigrants and the rootless low-paid are drawn by cheap housing.

Rue Blaes and Rue Haute run parallel right through the district, and are arguably the oldest streets in Brussels. The heart of the Marolles is **Place du Jeu de Balle/Vossenplein** (off Rue Blaes), where 'brown cafés' and junk shops surround the square with its morning flea market.

The Gothic church of **Notre-Dame de la Chapelle/ Kapellekerk** marks the northern edge of the Marolles. The Flemish master Pieter Bruegel the Elder is buried beneath its huge belltower, and is thought to have lived at nearby 132 Rue Haute. There's a memorial to him in the church, made by his son Jan Brueghel.

There's another side to the Marolles today, as late-night bars and clubs attract a younger crowd, and chic, arty stores muscle in to share the atmosphere.

Louise/Louiza

Bus 34 goes from the Bourse to Place Louise. Trams 93 and 94 run along Avenue Louise.

In huge contrast to next-door Marolles, the smartest part of Brussels for living or shopping is Place Louise and Avenue Louise and the surrounding boulevards and streets. The area starts at the Palais de Justice law courts and heads along Avenue Louise. Here you'll find a mix of **designer stores** like Gucci, Versace and others rubbing shoulders with trashier elements like ice-cream parlours and fast-food diners. In smaller streets to either side, cafés and bars set out their tables.

Beyond Place Stéphanie, the avenue gets wider and busier and is less pleasant or diverse. Except for a wiggle to get round the calm and beautiful **Cambré abbey** in its gardens, about 2km further on, Avenue Louise is as straight as an arrow. Originally tree-lined, it was a typical piece of Léopold II's grand-scale urban landscaping. He had the Palais de Justice built in town, the elegant Bois de la Cambré parkland laid out on the southern edge of the city, and a majestic avenue named after his daughter to join the two.

Ixelles/Elsene

Bus 71 skirts Grand-Place, heads to Porte de Namur and runs the length of Chaussée d'Ixelles, through the heart of the Ixelles district.

Boulevard de Waterloo/Waterloolaan, part of the hectic city centre ring road, runs the 600m from Place Louise to Porte de Namur, another focal point for shoppers. This is the start of Ixelles, the big, vibrant student quarter which lies south from here. **Chaussée d'Ixelles/Elsene Steenweg** is the district's meandering main street. Off to left and right, crooked, winding side turns offer tempting bars, restaurants and shops.

" *A rare old city, with strange costumes and wonderful architecture.* "
William Thackeray,
Vanity Fair, 1848

Chaussée d'Ixelles ends at the two Ixelles lakes, beyond which **Brussels University** (divided into French and Flemish sections) creates a student area of inexpensive bars and restaurants.

Strangely, on the other side of Avenue Louise there's a detached part of Ixelles which is quieter, merging into the Art Nouveau district, **St Gilles**.

Parc du Cinquantenaire/ Jubelpark

East of the city centre. Park entrances: Rue de la Loi and Avenue de Tervueren. Metro: Mérode or Schuman. Tram: 81, 82. Bus: 20, 28, 36, 61, 67, 80.

To celebrate Belgium's 50th anniversary (*cinquantenaire* in French, *jubel* in Flemish), in the 1880s Léopold II proudly

created an immense park and placed in it a palace of museums and a soaring triumphal arch topped with extravagant symbolic statues to the glory of Belgium. It was just one of the many urban projects which King Léopold conceived to put Belgium firmly on the world map – with great success. In fact, the 1897 World Fair was staged in this park. The park continued to develop and Léopold's vision was not fully realised until after World War I.

Le Cinquantenaire today is a pleasing area of calm, walks and greenery close to the city centre, popular for a family outing, with a play area, though at night it is considered dangerous. The large **museums** remain important (though it's wise to concentrate on a few key exhibits), and there's plenty to see and visit in the park. However, much of the grandeur has been whittled away, as in 1974 when the city authorities ran an expressway through the middle of it, partly as underpasses.

Royal Museums of Art and History

Inside park. Tel: 741 7211. Open Tue–Fri 0930–1700; weekends and national hols, 1000–1700. Admission: ££.

Ancient artworks dominate this vast complex, one of Europe's largest museums. Stuffed with archaeological finds and antiquities from around the world, together with a section on Belgian prehistory, the museum has some 140 rooms, and cultural and educational resources ranging from children's workshops to a research library of 100,000 books. One area is designated a **museum for the blind**, where the visually impaired can use hands and ears, not eyes, to discover the past.

Key exhibits include 3000–5000-year-old metal and earthenware artwork from the Near East (Level 0); an intriguing model of Rome at the time of Emperor Constantine (Level 0); a 16th-century Indian feather cloak from Brazil (Level 1); an Easter Island statue (Level 1); a lovely statue of a boy in Art Deco style called *The Mysterious Sphinx*, by Van der Stappen in 1897 (Level 1); Roman statuary and mosaics (Level 2); the relief portrait of Queen Tiy of about 1400 BC.

Autoworld

Inside Park. Tel: 736 4165. Open 1000–1700 (Apr–Oct, 1000–1800). Admission: ££.

The biggest crowd-puller in the Cinquantenaire Park is the sort of thing that would have been furthest from King Léopold's thoughts. Adjacent to the Art and History Museum is an outstanding collection of nearly 500 motor vehicles from the 1880s to the 1980s. Most were acquired from the Ghislain Mahy Collection.

Great names and classic cars, such as the earliest Mercedes Benz and Ford Model T, stand alongside rarities and curiosities, among them Belgian cars such as a 1948 Imperia and a 1902 Minerva. You can get an overview without going in, by visiting the separate cafeteria.

Rest of the park

Elsewhere within the palace there's a (rather dry) **Museum of the Army and Military History** (*tel: 733 4493. Open Mon–Fri 0900–1200, 1300–1700; Sat, Sun 1000–1700. Free*). The most interesting section deals thoroughly with the 1830 Revolution. Another highlight is part of the museum devoted to aircraft and aviation, with displays of Great War and World War II fighters, as well as more recent planes and helicopters.

❝ *Of all the peoples of Gaul, the Belgians are the bravest.* **❞**

Julius Caesar

The early Art Nouveau **Human Passions Pavilion** designed by Horta stands in one corner of the park, and has become a monument to prudery. Opened in 1899 to house a relief fresco of the same name by Jef Lambeaux, it was closed after just a few days because Lambeaux's uninhibited work was considered offensive, and has never reopened. You can look through an opening to see what all the fuss was about.

Euro-Brussels

The European insitutions are located around Parc Léopold and Rond-Point Schuman, west of Parc du Cinquantenaire. Metro: Schuman. Bus (from city centre): 20, 38. No trams.

For people around the world, the name Brussels is synonymous with the European Union. It started in 1957 with the signing of the Treaty of Rome, which set up the **European Economic Community** with its original six Member States, who jointly decided Brussels would be their capital. The next year they created Euratom, to develop and promote nuclear power, the first of many Europe-wide political bodies to be based in Brussels.

As the European institutions clustered and grew here, they demanded prestigious premises to match their autocratic self-importance. Quartier Léopold, the lively, pretty area next to Parc du Cinquantenaire, was demolished to make way for the huge EU building project, which continues today.

Busy Rue de la Loi and Rue Belliard run between the European buildings, which do project an aura of power and a sense that armies of civil servants are toiling industriously. Around 20,000 people are employed in this quarter by the European Union.

Look out for the 11-storey Résidence Palace at 155 Rue de la Loi, an Art Nouveau survival.

Centre Berlaymont

Rond-Point Schumann. Not open to public.

One of the most extraordinary structures anywhere is the vast asbestos-ridden folly constructed by the new European Economic Community in one of its earliest money-no-object gestures. The huge Berlaymont structure, in the shape of a slightly off-centre crucifix, housed the first generation of

Eurocrats and civil servants. Because of the asbestos problem, the Berlaymont had to be evacuated in 1991 and sealed up within a cloth covering, giving it the appearance of a gigantic, and enigmatic, open-air art object. For many, it remains the symbol of the European bureaucracy, with crowds gathering here for protests and demonstrations.

European Parliament

Rue du Remorqueur, off Rue Belliard. To enquire about visiting, call 284 3457.

The sheer cost, size and opulence of the European Parliament and its administrative support building, opened in 1998, enraged many. Combining rigid straight lines with formal curves, they are beautiful examples of modern architecture, the predominant material being glass. The Parliament cannot be visited except by prior arrangement, which is generally possible for groups but not usually individuals.

Parc Léopold

Main entrance: Rue Belliard.

The soaring new EU buildings have turned this park into a tiny scrap of greenery amidst the glass and concrete.

79

Who runs Europe?

The Council of Ministers: **Based in Brussels, this is Europe's ultimate decision-making body.**

The European Commission: **Based mainly in Brussels, this is the EU's 17 non-elected independent Commissioners who draw up European legislation and manage all European funding, together with some 10,000 administration staff and civil servants.**

The European Parliament: **Based in Strasbourg, but located in Brussels three weeks out of every four, this is the forum for the 567 elected members.**

The European Court: **Based in Luxembourg.**

The Auditors: **Based in Luxembourg.**

West Brussels

*The main attractions are at **Heysel**, a plateau in the northwest of Brussels, a large part of which has been laid out as a recreation and leisure district. The Heysel Stadium, scene of the 1985 European Champions Cup final tragedy in which scores of spectators died in an outbreak of football hooliganism, is here. It has been extensively redesigned since then and renamed Stade Roi Baudoin (King Baudoin Stadium).*

Atomium

Boulevard du Centenaire, Laeken. Tel: 477 0977. Metro: Heysel. Tram: 81. Open 0900–1700 (Apr–Aug), 1000–1800 (Sept–Mar). Admission: ££.

This bizarre attraction is one of the best-known images of Brussels. A structure of nine linked silver spheres, it was erected for the 1958 World Fair (the second time Brussels had hosted the Fair) to symbolise a new 'atomic age'. It might be mistaken for a work of art, but accurately depicts an iron molecule – magnified 165 billion times.

It's huge: each aluminium and steel sphere measures 18m across, the linking tubes are 29m long, and the top sphere stands 102m above the ground. Even more amazing, escalators run between the spheres, three of which can be entered, each containing two storeys. Four of them house long-term exhibitions. A high-speed lift travels at 5m/s taking just 23 seconds to reach the Atomium's top sphere. This highest level moves by as much as 50cm in the breeze, contains a warm and convivial **restaurant** and gives an incomparable view over Brussels and the countryside beyond.

“ *Our country has the unique advantage of lying at the crossroads of the great cultures of Europe.* ”

King Baudouin I of the Belgians

Mini-Europe and Bruparck

Bruparck, 20 Boulevard du Centenaire Laeken. Tel: 478 0550. Metro: Heysel.
Tram: 81, 91, 18, 19. Open 0930–1800 (Apr–June), 0930–2000 (1–19 July,
20–31 Aug), 0930–2400 (20 July–19 Aug), 1000–1800 (1 Sept–6 Jan). Closed
6 Jan–31 Mar. Admission: £££.

Beside Atomium lies Bruparck, the city's 25-hectare family leisure park, with a multitude of amusements and attractions. All Brussels kids are brought here to see films at **Kinepolis**, a 27-cinema complex which includes a vast all-round Imax screen. There's a planetarium, a popular water activity park called L'Océade, and many cheap and cheerful eating places clustered together in 'The Village'.

The main interest for visitors is **Mini-Europe**, an enjoyable, frivolous display of some the most famous and symbolic buildings of the countries belonging to the European Union. Everything is exactly reduced to $^1/_{25}$th of its real size – except the Eiffel Tower, which is smaller. Belgians insist there is nothing political in this.

81

Basilique du Sacré-Coeur/Basiliek van het Heilig Hart

Sacred Heart Basilica (Koekelberg Basilica) 2km south of Heysel. 1 Parvis de la
Basilique, Koekelberg. Tel: 425 8822. Metro: Simonis. Bus: 87. Open Apr–Sept
0800–1800, Oct–Mar 0800–1700. Free.

Another amazing viewpoint across the city from this immense, lofty basilica modelled on the Sacré-Coeur in Paris and dedicated to the same Catholic cult. But the comparison stops there – Koekelberg is not Montmartre, and this basilica is concrete, sandstone and red-brick, not gleaming white. King Léopold decided to build it in 1902, but the structure wasn't started until three years later, and not completed until 1970. There are interesting modern **stained-glass windows** and some fine **statuary**, but the main attraction remains the sheer size and impressive view.

Eating and drinking

Cafés and bars

Heysell

The Village in Bruparck is the eating and drinking section, with a big choice.

Louise

The busy Avenue Louise/Porte de Namur area has many bars and brasseries to choose from, including:

L'Atelier de la Truffe Noir

300 Avenue Louise. Tel: 640 5455. Open 0830–1900 Mon–Sat. ££. Spare, elegant, chic, this could be classed as just a bar, just a tearoom, or just a patisserie, but it also serves first-class sandwiches and light meals, some of them very luxurious and expensive (eg those with truffles).

Cybertheatre

4–5 Avenue de la Toison d'Or. Tel: 500 7811. Open Sun–Thur 1000–0100, Fri–Sat 1000–0200. ££. Eat, drink and surf the net at this large theatre-style cybercafé, where there are often evening events.

Rick's Bar

344 Avenue Louise. Tel: 647 7530. Open 1100–2400. ££. This American place is a Brussels institution, full of Americans living and working in the city, as well as tourists. Specialises in good cocktails, has a pleasant walled garden and food all day.

Marolles

This area has low-priced neighbourhood bars, alternative cafés and noisy late-night places. For a drink, snack or meal at any time of day or night, look around Place Jeu de Balle.

Indigo

160 Rue Blaes. Tel: 511 3897. Open Tue–Fri 1000–1500, Sat–Sun 0930–1600. £. Just right for a salad and quiche lunch or some home-made cake and tea, and furnished with bargains from the nearby daily junk market.

Ixelles and St Gilles

Ordinary bars in ordinary streets are the rule here, with plenty of youthful, beer-loving places close to the university and smarter establishments by the lakes.

L'Atelier

77 Rue Elise. Tel: 649 1953. Open 1800–0300. £. Noisy, popular student bar near the university, big choice of beers and often live music.

Moeder Lambic

68 Rue de Savoie. Tel: 539 1419. Open 1600–0400. £. Lambic is one of the principal styles of Belgian beer, so this little place is really called 'Mother Beer'. That's fair, as they reckon to serve 1000 varieties. It's a couple of streets south of the Horta Museum.

La Porteause d'Eau

48 Avenue Jean Volders. Tel: 538 8354. Open 1000–0100. £. Lovers of Art Nouveau wandering the streets around St Gilles before or after visiting the Horta Museum might be glad to find this restored Art Nouveau local bar not far from St Gilles church.

Cinquantenaire and European Quarter

There are refreshments inside the museums.

Wild Geese

24 Avenue Livingstone. Tel: 230 1990. Open 1100–0100. £. Just a few paces north of the principal European institutions, this Irish pub is a favourite after-hours hangout of Euro officials and their staff.

Restaurants

Heysel

Adrienne

Atomium Square Atomium. Tel: 478 3000. Closed Sun, 3 weeks in July and a week at Christmas. £. The circular restaurant at the top of Atomium is popular not just for the view but for its good all-you-want buffet at modest prices.

Louise

L'Amadeus

13 Rue Veydt. Tel: 538 3427. Tue–Sat 1200–1530, 1830–0200. ££. This atmospheric wine bar and restaurant off Rue Defacqz (off Avenue Louise) has candles and dark or bare-brick interiors and is in what used to be the studio of sculptor Auguste Rodin. Good wines by the glass, and good food too, including oysters and local specialities like *waterzooi* stew.

Marolles

L'Idiot du Village

19 Rue Notre-Seigneur. Tel: 502 5582. Open Mon–Fri 1200–1400, 1930–2300. £££. At the top end of Marolles, down a backstreet near the church, this classic little restaurant is prettily decorated and furnished.

Noche Latina

204 Rue Haute. Tel: 502 0199. Open for lunch, and dinner till late. £. There are plenty of low-cost places to choose from along Rue Haute and Rue Blaes, quite a lot of them foreign. This one offers South American food, people and music, in a warm, animated atmosphere.

Ixelles/St Gilles

Dolma

329 Chaussée d'Ixelles. Tel: 649 8991. Open Mon–Sat 1200–1400, 1900–2200. ££. Useful pure vegetarian eatery attached to a health-food shop. Good value.

Raconte Moi Des Salades

19 Place du Châtelain. Tel: 534 2727. Open Mon–Sat 1200–1500, 1900–0100. £. Moderately priced restaurants cluster around the Place du Chatelain area, off Avenue Louise (on the west side). This one, called Tell Me About Salads, offers plenty of other things too, including omelettes and pasta dishes. Outside tables.

Shopping

Fashion and Souvenirs

Avenue Louise and **Porte de Namur Boulevard de Waterloo**, which runs between them, and the small side streets and covered lanes called *galeries* (especially around Porte de Namur), form the principal Brussels shopping district, especially for department stores, luxuries, designer fashions and accessories and upmarket specialist outlets. **Galeries de la Toison d'Or**, **Chaussée d'Ixelles** and **Chaussée de Wavre**, south and east from Porte de Namur, are a more affordable shopping option.

Designers located here include **Versace** (*61 Boulevard de Waterloo*), Belgian top names, such as **Gerard Watelet** (*268 Avenue Louise*) and **Thierry Mugler** (*80 Avenue Louise*), and Spanish designer **Adolfo Dominguez** (*118 Avenue Louise*).

Food and drink

La Truffe Noir (*300 Avenue Louise, open 1000–1900 Mon–Sat*) is the poshest of gourmet delicatessens.

Bière Artisanale (*174 Chaussée de Wavre, open 1100–1900, Mon–Sat*) has a phenomenal range of 'real ale', Belgian style, as well as all the right glasses. They do beer tastings, as well.

Antiques and Secondhand

Thanks to its fascinating daily **bric-à-brac market** in **Place Jeu de Balle** (*0700–1400, some stalls closing earlier*), the **Marolles** district has become a place to search for antiques, secondhand goods and period furniture bargains. Among the butchers, bakers and ordinary shops of this residential neighbourhood, there are several antique dealers. Among the interesting variations are **Idiz Bogam** (*162 Rue Blaes*), selling wonderful vintage clothing, and **La Fiancée du Pirate** (*118 Rue Blaes*), with a fascinating array of old seafaring paraphernalia.

Gifts

Serneels (*69 Avenue Louise, open 0930–1800, Mon–Sat*) is a terrific toy shop, with a huge array of goodies kids may not have seen at home.

La Maison du Bridge (*64 Rue du Bailli, open 1000–1300, 1330–1830, Tue–Sat*). Not just bridge, but every board game imaginable and accoutrements like mats, tables, etc.

Clubs and nightlife

Démence and D-Light

208 Rue Blaes. Open 2300–0600 or later. Entrance fee. The city has a big gay and lesbian scene, with several venues. This is the biggest and most popular, a wild once-monthly disco, dance and dressing-up affair: last Sun in month at Démence (for men), last Fri in month at D-Light (women).

The Fuse

208 Rue Blaes. Open every Sat, 2300–0600 or later. Entrance fee. Huge teen crowds for weekly hit of Techno. Also hosts gay Démence and D-Light (*see above*).

Theatres and Cinemas

UGC Acropole

17 Galerie de la Toison d'Or and 8 Avenue de la Toison d'Or. Tel: 0900 10440. This major 11-screen cinema complex shows a full range of Hollywood hits and obscure French favourites. You need to know if it's VO (version original, not dubbed) or ST (subtitled).

Kinepolis at Bruparck

Booking: 474 2600; info in French: 0900 35241. With 29 screens, this is the place to see either new mainstream releases or, for a memorable film experience, an Imax movie. Perfect for kids, and the place is filled with them.

Brussels to put banana battle before WTO

Brussels plans to take legal action against Washington over a US threat to impose punitive tariffs against European exports. The counter-threat of retaliation from the European Commission further increases the chance that the phoney 'banana war' could turn into a full-scale trade conflict. Fears are growing that Washington's determination to fight the EU's discrimination against Central American bananas might lead to tit-for-tat tariffs.

The Times, 12 November 1998. An example of how Brussels is shorthand not for Belgium but for the whole of Europe

Art Nouveau

*Tragically, the city of Brussels has demolished large numbers of the finest Art Nouveau structures ever built. Public protest, and a dawning awareness that this ornate, forward-looking and imaginative turn-of-the-century architecture had a following, only recently persuaded the municipality to adopt a new attitude. The change of heart is clear from the restoration of the Old England department store, which was scheduled to be demolished but instead has been earmarked to rehouse the city's Musical Instrument Museum (*see page 59*).*

Brussels remains one of the two pre-eminent cities of Art Nouveau (the other is Vienna), and benefited from the presence of Victor Horta, one of the originators and masters of the style. Lasting from the 1890s to World War I, Art Nouveau was a self-consciously modern movement for a new century. It made extensive use of glass and metal (especially steel and wrought iron), and favoured craftsmanship, illumination and abundant clean-lined decoration. A distinctive feature of many Art Nouveau buildings, whether private houses, business premises or large public buildings, is the use of interior daylight admitted through a 'well of light' at the centre.

As well as the Old England store (*see page 59*), don't miss the Cartoon-Strip Centre (*see page 53*). Maison de St Cyr (*Square Ambiorix*) is one of several Art Nouveau houses in Square Ambiorix and Square Marie-Louise, just north of the European Institutions, and in Avenue Palmerston, running between the two squares, particularly Nos 2, 3, and especially 4 (*Hôtel van Eetvelde*).

The Ixelles, Uccle and St Gilles districts have many smaller examples, such as the houses at 19 and 21 Rue Vanderschrick; Hôtel Solvay (*224 Avenue Louise*); 71, 48 and 50 Rue Defacqz and Victor Horta's first work, Hôtel Tassel, at 6 Rue Janson (both off Avenue Louise). These districts, especially **St Gilles**, were being constructed as the city expanded at the end of the 19th century. Many building plots were bought by left-wing bourgeois families, who employed Art Nouveau architects to design statements of their radicalism.

Musée Horta/Victor Horta Museum

23–25 Rue Américaine. Tel: 537 1692. Open 1400–1730. Closed Mon and national hols. Admission: ££ weekdays, £££ weekends.

Among the surviving Art Nouveau buildings, the supreme example of a domestic interior in the style, is Victor Horta's own St Gilles home and next-door studio. The house has become a museum of Art Nouveau, with a perfect harmony of design, using glass, iron and wall-painting. Horta's claim to have personally designed 'every door hinge and door handle' is quite believable, every detail seemingly conceived

as part of the whole building. Some of the furnishings, however, were brought here from another Horta building, La Maison Dopchy, out of town at Renaix. These intruders can be recognised at once: everything in the original Horta residence was in the range yellow, pink, red or orange. The lampshades, rug, and items of any other colour were brought here from other houses.

BRUGES: The City's Heart

Bruges: The City's Heart

Medieval Bruges (Flemish: Brugge, pronounced 'Bruhe') was among the richest and busiest of towns. By an accident of history it became such a backwater that for centuries it remained unchanged. Then Bruges was discovered again, cleaned and polished, repaired and restored. Today its squares and lanes and canalside walks are among Europe's most treasured possessions, a perfect, storybook town of old Flanders.

Bruges:
The City's Heart

Getting there: If arriving in Bruges by train from Brussels, you'll need to catch a bus or cab from the station to the town centre. Almost all buses from the station go to Markt, the service is frequent, the drivers speak English, and the fare is under £1.

Coming by car from Brussels or Ostend, travel on motorway A10 (E40) and take exit 8 for Bruges. From Calais, travel via Ostend.

① Markt

The centre of everything, and the perfect spot to admire Flemish architecture from the comfort of an outdoor café table. The historic market square is surrounded by fine old buildings, the ground floors of many having been transformed into restaurants and bars serving an array of Belgian beers and local dishes. **Pages 92–93**

② Go up the Belfry

The massive brick Halletoren towering over Markt fills the square with the sound of carillon bells every 15 minutes and is the town centre's principal landmark. The covered market and Belfry form a fine complex around a small courtyard, and from the top there's no better the view over the roofs and gables. **Pages 94–95**

③ Burg

Just stand and stare in this exquisite square. Adjacent to Markt, it's smaller, quieter, and dominated by exceptional public buildings – the ancient Romanesque basilica, the Flamboyant-Gothic town hall, and the public record office in Renaissance style. You can pick up a horsedrawn carriage here. **Pages 96–97**

④ Heilig Bloedbasiliek (Holy Blood Basilica)

Strange name, strange church. Built after the Second Crusade to hold a venerated phial of what the pious believe is Christ's blood, the Basilica's dark interior is oddly shaped, juxtaposes architectural styles and possesses a powerful atmosphere. **Page 97**

⑤ Diamonds

Diamond-polishing has been a Belgian speciality since the Middle Ages – and it all started in Bruges before shifting to Antwerp. Visit the new Diamond Museum to learn more, or even buy a few to take home. **Page 98**

⑥ Old Masters

The paintings of the Flemish Primitives found their way all over medieval Europe, as much in demand as other Flemish arts and crafts. The Groeninge and Memling art museums have exceptional collections of these works, and more accessible than in almost any other town. **Pages 98–99**

Tip

Even if you have come by car, don't try driving around the town. Traffic restrictions, barriers, one-ways and no-parking zones are designed to make life hard for the motorist. On the other hand, it's easy for pedestrians and cyclists – so join them. There are several large car parks, indicated by blue and white 'P' illuminated road signs which also show if there if space available.

Tourist information

The town's tourist office is in Burg square. *VVV/Toerisme Brugge, Burg 11. Tel: 050 44 86 86; fax: 050 44 86 00.*

91

Markt

The cheerful traffic-free bustle of Markt (or Grote Markt), the lovely cobbled main square at the centre of Bruges, with its stream of cyclists, its horsedrawn tourist carriages, the massive brick Belfry and a fine gathering of gables on a dozen seafood restaurants and bars, makes a perfect starting point for a visit to the town. Yet it's also a base which constantly beckons you to return – for a meal, a drink, or simply to admire the typical old Flemish buildings on all four sides.

Bruges has nearly 3 million visitors annually, making it Belgium's premier tourist attraction. Most stay less than a day, though Bruges welcomes over a million overnight guests each year. Almost all visitors spend part of their visit in Markt. By contrast the total population of Bruges and its surrounding villages is about 120,000.

The bright energy of the square belies just how much more lively it must have been in former days. Every week from the year 1200 to 1983, an open-air market was held here. And more than just the principal market. Through the ages Markt was a public rallying place, where protests were voiced, proclamations made and executions carried out.

For most visitors, Markt remains the highlight of this most congenial of towns. Beautiful during the day, it's magical at night, when spotlights capture the detail on the historic façades.

Many of the buildings are former guildhalls. The **Provinciaal Hof**, in neo-Gothic style, is the West Flanders government house and, together with the **Post Office**, stands on the site of the old Waterhalles where boats once moored. Until 1787, this covered harbour brought trading ships right into the market-place.

The southern side of the square is a bit of romantic pastiche, where modern buildings in medieval style stand alongside authentic old houses. However, all blend effectively together in harmony.

The statue in the centre of the square shows **Jan Breydel** (a butcher) and **Pieter de Coninck** (a one-eyed weaver), leaders of the 1302 Brugse Metten (Bruges Morning) uprising during which local people massacred the French garrison stationed here. This developed into the Battle of the Golden Spurs, an iconic moment in the Flemish national story, when ordinary Flemish people won a resounding victory against a force of French knights sent to quell them.

The uprising followed a year after the Burgundian Duke Philip the Handsome had taken control of Bruges. Philip's duchess, Queen Joan of Navarre, complained that the women of Bruges wore such fine clothes and jewellery that she felt she could see 'hundreds of queens' where she should be the only one.

When the Flemish rebelled against growing French influence, the town was torn between pro-French aristocratic Leliarts (Lily People – ie the French *fleur de lys*, or lily flower) and the anti-French Clauwearts (Claw People), who were said to kill anyone who could not pronounce Flemish correctly.

Hallen en Belfort
(Covered Market and Belfry)

A distinctive feature of Flemish towns is the landmark Belfry, rising from a civic building rather than a church. The tallest belfry in Belgium rises high above Markt, and above the rooftops of Bruges. Symbolic of the power of commerce, the towering brick Belfry soars from the old covered Cloth Market next to the square. Dwarfing the market-place, it seems somehow disproportionately massive, much too tall and too wide for the setting. A decorative octagonal crown was put in place in 1486, and in those days the Belfry was even taller, as a lofty wooden spire rose from the top; burnt down in 1741, the spire was not replaced.

BRUGES: The City's Heart

The Belfry's carillon, with 47 bells, rings out every 15 minutes, and about three times a week complete concerts are played on these steeple bells. *Concerts: June–Sept Mon, Wed and Sat at 2100, and Sun at 1415. Rest of year Wed and Sat or Sun at 1415.*

Built over a 200-year period (13th–15th centuries), the immense bell tower originally served as a treasury, where the city's valuables were securely stored – items such as the town's gold reserves and royal charters were stored here.

To look inside, pass through the archway beneath the Belfry into a courtyard of dark grey-red brick and cobblestone, enclosed by the **Cloth Market** where in medieval times hundreds of merchants gathered to buy and sell the famous Bruges woollen cloth, tapestries, weaving and lace. Steps lead into the **Belfry**. For those with the determination, it is possible to climb a winding staircase of 366 steps to the very top, 88m high. From here the view extends far beyond the town, giving a geographer's eye-view of the waterways, swinging around the old heart of Bruges and heading out to the North Sea.

Reaching the top section, pause to look at the impressive bells and carillon mechanism, a huge copper drum made in 1748. It's considered one of the finest **carillons** in the world. If you're here at the right moment, try to catch a glimpse as the hour strikes: big concrete hammers crash onto the bells with a deafening reverberation. Most visitors don't get that far, preferring to stop at the Belfry's second storey, in the Middle Ages the town's treasure-room, today a museum.

Markt 7. Tel: 405 6111. Open Apr–Sept 0930 –1700 daily, Oct–Mar 0930–1230 and 1330–1700 daily. Admission: ££ (family ticket £).

" *In the market place of Bruges stands the Belfry old and brown;*
Thrice consumed and thrice rebuilded, still it watches o'er the town.
As the summer morn was breaking, on that lofty tower I stood,
And the world threw off the darkness like the weeds of widowhood. "

H W Longfellow, '*The Belfry of Bruges*', 1845

Burg

Touching the main square at one corner, the calmer neighbouring square, Burg, is a smaller, more subdued space where horsedrawn carriages wait for hire.

It is enclosed by an even more striking ensemble of Flemish architecture. If picturesque Markt represents medieval trade and merchant power, Burg – the name means 'castle' –

symbolises the even greater powers of city, state and church. That's why, during those times, and until the 18th century, Burg was protected by high walls and locked gates. Once upon a time, there was a real castle here, built by Count Baldwin to protect the town from Vikings, but that disappeared long ago.

However, the square has changed a great deal in the last 200 years. Much of its appearance today dates from a period of neo-Gothic construction and reconstruction at the turn of the 18th century, when St Donatian's 10th-century church was demolished (a fragment remains in the gardens on the north side of the square). Burg's highlight is the Flamboyant-Gothic **town hall** of 1376, a bright drapery of lacy white stonework along one side of the square. Next to it, the old **Public Record Office** exemplifies the Renaissance, the former **Court of Justice** is neo-Classical, while on the other corner of the square, the exotic, galleried, almost oriental-looking **Steeghere**, entrance to the Basilica of the Holy Blood, is a looming, magical presence.

Stadhuis (Town Hall)

Tel: 050 33 99 11. Open Apr–Sept 0900–1700 daily; rest of year, exc Tue, 0930–1230, 1400–1700 daily. Admission: £.

Originally built in the 14th century, restored 500 years later, and given some new statues for the façade in the 1970s, this is one of the very grandest, most richly ornamented of all the many great Flemish town halls. Supremely elegant outwardly,

with its three perfectly spaced turrets and pale Gothic
stonework as delicate as old lace, it is just as good inside.
A grandiose staircase climbs to the Gothic Room, used
for formal receptions. It has a gorgeous ceiling, panelled
and vaulted, and Gothic-style wall paintings.

Heilig Bloedbasiliek (Holy Blood Basilica)

*Tel: 050 33 71 73. Open Apr–Sept 1000–1715 daily; rest of year 1000–1145,
1330–1615 daily. Admission: £.*

The Steeghere entrance porch visible from the square is like
the iceberg's tip. Steps lead from the entrance to the modest
church door. Inside, the Basilica is vast and complex. The
powerful dark, bare stone of the Basilica's crypt and Basilius
Chapel have all the sturdy simplicity of the Romanesque
style of the 12th century, when Thierry of Alsace, Count
of Flanders, returned to Bruges from the Second Crusade.
According to the official version of the legend, he had with
him a phial of blood obtained in Jerusalem from the Patriarch
of the Holy City, declaring that it was the genuine blood of
Jesus Christ. This great Basilica was built in its honour, a
perfect model of the ornamented and decorated Flemish
open-plan church. Later remodelled in Gothic style, and
with neo-Gothic additions in the 19th century, the hybrid
architecture seems to convey the endurance through
changing ages of the peoples' piety and devotion to the
strange relic.

97

On the first floor is the Chapel of the Holy Blood, with
its silver altar, and here the reliquary is kept. Made of rock
crystal encased with brilliant gold workmanship, it is now
known to have been made in Istanbul at about the time
Thierry obtained it, though the liquid inside has not been
tested. The Noble Brotherhood of the Holy Blood, formed to
protect and honour the relic, ride on horseback at the head
of the colourful and passionate Procession of the Holy Blood
through the town each May, locals following in medieval
costume and re-enacting Biblical scenes.

*The Holy Blood Procession takes place on Ascension Day each year
(13 May 1999, 1 June 2000). The programme is always as follows:
0830–1015: Veneration of the Relic in the Basilica of the Holy Blood;
1100: High Mass in St Saviour's Cathedral; 1500–1800: Procession of the
Holy Blood; 1800: Benediction and worship of the Relic in Burg square.*

The museums

Bruges likes to think of itself as a 'city of museums'. Officially, there are more than 30 of them in the little town, including unmuseum-like historic sights such as the Belfry, the Gothic Room in the City Hall, the Lace Centre and the breweries. In addition, churches make up much of the town's storehouse of medieval treasures.

Brangwynmuseum/Arentshuis

16 Dijver. Tel: 050 448763. Open 0930–1700, exc Tue; Oct–Mar closed for lunch 1230–1400. Admission: £.

Lovely landscapes of Bruges and surrounding country, together with a collection of the finest old lacework, and all sorts of memorabilia of historic Bruges, are displayed in this exquisite 18th-century town house. The first floor is devoted to the decorative art of Frank Brangwyn, the English but Bruges-born pupil of William Morris who became an official World War I artist.

Diamantmuseum (Diamond Museum)

93 Katelijnestraat (Ankerplaats). Tel: 050 34416. Open Mon–Fri 1000–1200, 1300–1700, Sat 1000–1500. Admission: £.

The history of diamond-polishing in Bruges had been all but forgotten until recently, even though this important Belgian industry was well established in Bruges long before shifting to Antwerp. It's all explained in this fascinating museum.

Groeninge Museum/Stedelijk Museum voor Schone Kunsten

12 Dijver. Tel: 050 448750. Open 0930–1700, closed Tue and Sun. Admission: ££.

This is the main Bruges museum of fine art, with particularly fine collections of masterpieces by Flemish Primitives, notably Van Eyck, Memling, Pieter Brueghel the Younger and a small painting by Hieronymus Bosch.

Gruuthusemuseum

17 Dijver. Tel: 050 448762. Open 0930–1700, closed Tue and Sun. Admission: ££.

Originally a luxurious private mansion built by Louis de Bruges, then a place for buying and selling *gruut*, a base of flowers, herbs and barley used in brewing, the Gruuthuse now serves as a museum of decorative arts. It preserves hundreds of examples of the arts and crafts of Flanders from the Middle Ages to modern times.

Memling Museum

Sint Janshospitaal, 38 Mariastraat. Tel: 050 448770. Open 0930–1700, closed Tue and Sun. Admission: £.

Though German by birth, Hans Memling lived and worked in Bruges and his painting became strongly associated with the town. He donated paintings to this 15th-century hospital, which now possesses six of his works, including *The Mystical Marriage of St Catherine* tritych and *The Reliquary of St Ursula*.

Onze-Lieve-Vrouwekerk (Church of Our Lady)

Onze-Lieve-Vvrouwekerkhof Zuid. Tel: 050 448686. Open Apr–Sept Mon–Fri 1000–1130, 1430–1700, Sat closes an hour earlier, Sun afternoons only; rest of year Mon–Fri 1000–1130, 1430–1630, Sat closes 30 min earlier, Sun afternoon only. Admission: £.

One of the landmark spires of Bruges rises from this Gothic church, soaring 122m high and illuminated at night. Hanging amongst the ornate décor inside, there is a small painting of the Madonna and Child by Michelangelo – a rare sight outside his native Italy. The tombs of Mary of Burgundy and her father Charles the Bold lie in the chancel.

Cafés, bars and restaurants

Markt

Several inexpensive bar-brasseries on the north side of the central Markt square offer simple set tourist menus, typically soup, mussels and fries, and ice-cream. For the more adventurous, most also offer a few popular local specialities, especially *waterzooi*, the Flemish fish (sometimes chicken) stew. They're open all day long from about 0700 until around midnight.

Quick
14 Markt. Tel: 050 331979.

Craenenburg
16 Markt. Tel: 050 33 34 02.

Huyze Die Maene
17 Markt. Tel: 050 333959.

De Beurze
22 Markt. Tel: 050 335079.

La Taverne Brugeoise
27 Markt. Tel: 050 332132.

Sint-Joris
29 Markt. Tel: 050 333062.

De Gouden Meermin
31 Markt. Tel: 050 333776.

La Civière d'Or
33 Markt. Tel: 050 343036.

Around the town centre

Cafedraal
38 Zilverstraat. Tel: 050 340845. Open 1130–0200, closed Sun and Mon. ££. Food only available at mealtimes. Inside, interesting 15th-century building with enclosed inner courtyard.

Chagall
40 Sint-Amandstraat. Tel: 050 336112. Open 1100–2330 daily. ££. Likeable, civilised bar and restaurant noted for good seafood.

Den Dijver
5 Dijver. Tel: 050 336069. Lunch and dinner, closed Wed. ££. Relaxed, atmospheric old-fashioned canalside place specialising in dishes cooked with beer, a Flemish tradition.

De Gouden Harynck
25 Groeninge. Tel: 050 337637. Lunch and dinner, closed Sun, Mon. £££. One of the best of Bruges' many restaurants. Imaginative cooking but traditional décor of old Bruges. Close to Memling Museum.

Tom Pouce
17 Burg. Tel: 050 330336. Open all day, every day. ££. Touristy but enticing big tearoom, bar and restaurant in Burg, beside the Basilica entrance.

Shopping

The main shopping street is Steenstraat, leading off Markt. This continues into Zuidzandstraat, with more stores.

Thanks to the tourist trade, Bruges is one of the easiest places to buy Flemish specialities like chocolates, lace and the large Belgian biscuits called *speculoos* (cinnamon-flavoured biscuits in human form). The town is a shoppers' delight, with many large and small outlets selling the best of traditional craftsmanship.

Lace

Several shop windows are full of delicate handmade fine lace, ranging from affordable doilies and placemats to sumptuous dresses and shawls. **Gruuthuse** (*Dijver 15; open 1000– 1830, till 1900 in summer*). Sells high-quality lace, including antique; **Kantjuweeltje** (*Philipstockstraat 11; open 0900–1800, till 1900 in summer*). Has a wide range of new and old lace.

Fine chocolates and confectionery

Chocolatiers lay out their handmade wares like gold and silver jewellery. Others take a more robust attitude, and aim for a more down-to-earth style. At **Pralinette** (*31B Wollestraat; tel: 050 348444; open 0900–1900*), you can watch chocolates and pralines being made, as mouthwatering aromas waft from big melting cauldrons. Other good choc shops include: **The Chocolate Line** (*Simon Stevinplein; open Mon –Sat, 1000–1900*); **Depla** (*13 Huidenvettersplein; open 1000–1830*). **Sweertvaegher** (*29 Philipstockstraat; open 0930–1830, Closed Sun and Mon*).

Delicatessen and drinks

Deldycke (*23 Wollestraat; open 0900–1400, 1500–1830, closed Tue*) and **Woolstreet Company** (*31a Woollestraat; open 1000–1900*). Sells cheeses, *charcuterie* and speciality beers.

Other good buys

Brugs Diamanthuis (*5 Cordoeanierstraat; open Mon– Fri 1000–1200, 1330–1700, Sat 1000–1500*). Offers a range of diamond jewellery; **De Striep** (*42 Katelijnestraat; open Tue–Sat 1000–1230, 1330–1900. Mon pm only*). Wide selection of comics and cartoons.

Markets

Dijver Antiques and Secondhand *Dijver. Open Apr–Sept, Sat and Sun.* This canalside market looks like a flea market, but genuine antiques can be found.

Flemish Masters

The great Flemish towns– Bruges, Brussels, Ghent, Antwerp – proudly display their art heritage, remnants of Flanders' creative golden age. All have their fine art museums, and the best known of the Old Masters are all here – Jan Van Eyck, Pieter Breughel, Rogier Van Der Weyden, Hans Memling, Hugo Van Der Goes, Pieter-Paul Rubens, and his pupils Anthony Van Dyck and Jacob Jordaens, and more.

The **Flemish Primitives** were artists of the 14th and 15th centuries who turned away from respectful religious themes to an earthier love of the everyday. Their art developed out of the illustration and illumination of manuscripts, for which Flanders was already acclaimed. With the onset of the Renaissance, this tradition was continued, though modified, by 16th and 17th-century Flemish painters.

BRUGES: The City's Heart

The appeal is as much sociological as artistic. The sheer detail of the works gives a photo-crisp view of hairstyles and hats, dresses of exquisite cloth, ornate jewellery, heavy embroideries and cloaks – and did gentlemen really wear those enormous, suggestively shaped codpieces? **Facial expressions** are shown with poignant clarity. We see the sadness of 16th-century ladies, the furrowed, troubled brows of powerful men. Peasants are depicted – by the bourgeois artists – as lusty, uncouth, vivid beings, nearly animal in their physicality, the bodies muscular, their skin rosy as ripe fruit. Beer splashes from the jug, folk instruments are vigorously played, voices yell out, babies' bottoms are wiped with clothing, couples fondle one another.

In addition to this secular view, religious subjects were still popular, but with a similar vivid force. In an intensely devout age, the theology of the Flemish painters was that since every detail of the material world was God's work, depicting it as accurately as possible was a form of prayer, a way of honouring the creator. Usually, the religion of Flemish Primitives combined Christian mythology with meticulously **realistic scenes** of their own world. Thus, Rubens' Christ, blood pouring red, is taken from the cross by blond, Flemish-looking heroes.

Bruges: Around the City

Not only the two historic main squares at its centre, but the whole of old Bruges within its water gates, enclosed by the Reien waterway, is like some dreamy medieval artwork through which you can wander at will. Beyond the town too, travel along the Reie to Damme, where cargo ships moored in the Middle Ages.

BRUGES: Around the City

BEST OF

Bruges: Around the City

Getting there: All the places described are easily accessible from the town centre by foot, bus, horsedrawn carriage or taxi. One of the most enjoyable options is to hire a bicycle. The tourist office lists several bike hire companies.

① Lace

Handmade Flemish lace has been sought after for centuries, and is still the best, among the most expensive, and hardest to find. One of the easiest places to buy it is in Bruges, where finery once exclusive to aristocrats is now sold as souvenirs. Watch lace being made in the traditional way at the Kantcentrum – Bruges' lace centre. **Page 119**

② Beer

The many kinds of Belgian beer are easier to understand after a visit to one of the Bruges breweries and beer museums, like the Halve Maan (Half Moon) brewery in Walplein, and the Gouden Boom (Golden Tree) brewery in Langestraat. **Page 116**

③ Walk by the Minnewater

Legend and myth surrounds the swans floating peacfully on the picturesque Minnewater, alongside the Begijnhof. This is one of the most enjoyable little excursions in Bruges, whether you walk there or go by horse carriage. **Page 113**

④ Canal cruise

Even walking along the canalsides is a joy, their brick walls and stepped gables reflected shimmering in the dark water. More romantic still is a canalboat cruise, slowly cruising through the town centre on the historic waterways.

⑤ By water to Damme

Travelling by paddle-steamer slowly along the canalised river to the picturesque old harbour village of Damme makes a delightful interlude during a visit to Bruges. You could also walk there along the towpath – it's only 7km. **Pages 114–115**

⑥ Jeruzalemkerk district

On the east side of the town centre, the Jeruzalemkerk, St Anna Kerk, the Lace Centre and other sights stand in a neighbourhood which has kept a more authentic, less touristy atmosphere. **Pages 110–111**

A town for all seasons?

Bruges is beautiful enough that the crush of other tourists in summer and other holidays year round probably won't bother you. But if you can visit outside of usual holiday periods, you'll enjoy a calmer Bruges. Daffodil time, just before Easter, is especially pretty. May, between the Easter and summer breaks, is idyllic.

Tip

Bruges is an entirely Flemish-speaking town, and has a long history of fighting French domination, so don't bother to practise your school French here. Far better to use English – it's very widely spoken.

Canals

One of Bruges' greatest charms is the network of waterways encircling the historic centre. The dark waters flowing moodily below stone quays and canal paths, reflect the old brick walls, precipitously steep roofs with classic Flemish gables, ornate windows and flower-decked balconies. One of the most popular ways to explore the town is on a canal cruise, which gives a unique, delightful perspective. Just five families have the inherited, traditional right to run the cruises, each family operating four canalboats.

Not long ago, the canals were as busy as roads. Originally, the Reie river flowed through Bruges. Throughout the Middle Ages, as the town flourished and its cloth workers produced the finest fabrics and tapestries, new waterways were being created. These led off the Reie to the various shipyards and trading quays within the town. As time passed the Reie barely existed as a river any more; it had become a network of canals, known collectively as the Reien.

Ships used to enter the **Dampoort** city gate, and follow the **Langerei**, the branch of the river which heads into the centre. To reach the Waterhalles, they would turn right into the Spiegelrei branch, pausing at **Poortersloge**, the 15th-century 'Bourgeois Lodge' where nobility would gather for formal events. In front of it stands a statue of Jan Van Eyck, the great medieval Bruges painter. Now, the canal no longer exists at this point. It used to turn here into Markt, and continue to meet the Dijver branch of the Reien.

This flows up from the Minnewater (*see page 113*), past the Memling, Gruuthuse and Brangwyn museums (*see pages 98–99*), and beneath St John of Nepomuk bridge – named for the patron saint of bridges – to reach **Dijver** quay in the town centre. Here are picture-book views of towers and spires and bridges. The canal passes beneath the Woollestraat bridge, busy with cyclists and pedestrians, to **Rozenhoedkaai** (Rosary Quay) and the delightful quayside square **Huidenvettersplein** (Tanners' Square), which give exquisite views and perspectives. The lovely old building on the water's edge is the **Huidenvettershuis**, or Tanners' Guildhall – with scenes on the façade showing tanners at their work. Here the canal grandly turns a corner, and canalboats load and unload their cargoes of tourists: this is the principal starting point for a boat tour of the town. Just beyond is the 18th-century covered **Vismarkt**, or Fish Market, beside Burg square; here sea-fresh fish and shellfish are heaped and sold every morning, except Sun and Mon.

" *Crop-headed children spat upon us from the bridges, with a true conservative feeling. But even more conservative were the fishermen, who let us go by without one glance. They did not move any more than if they had been fishing in an old Dutch print.* "

Robert Louis Stevenson,
An Inland Voyage, **1876**

This arm of the Reien continues below Steenhouwersdijk to the Groene Rei quay, where waterways meet and the characteristic 18th-century Flemish charity hospital called **De Pelikaan** stands by the water.

Jeruzalemkerk Quarter

One arm of the Reien canals curves through the town from Sasplein to Gentpoort, creating a separate district on its east side. Here there's much to see in a pretty and unpretentious residential neighbourhood which keeps an authentic, less touristy atmosphere. There are bars, shops and cafés, but mainly geared to local people.

Getting there: a 10–15 min walk from Markt or Burg. Take Hoogstraat east, continue as it becomes Langestraat. Cross the canal bridge and turn left into Molenmeers to enter the quarter.

St Anna Kerk

Sint-Annaplein. Open Apr–Sept only.

Don't be fooled by the simple brick exterior. Look inside to discover a sumptuous 17th-century Gothic church adorned with exuberant Baroque pulpit, rood-screen and wood pannelling.

Jeruzalemkerk

Peperstraat. Open Mon–Fri 1000–1700, Sat 1000–1200.

This unusual privately owned church, with a strange lantern tower, may look familiar to some: it is modelled on the Holy Sepulchre in Jerusalem, hence the name. Pieter Adornes, ancestor of the present owners, constructed it after a 15th-century pilgrimage to the Holy Land. A century later, members of the family had themselves depicted in the stained-glass windows. Like the Holy Sepulchre, the building has three floors, with a Tomb of Christ in the crypt.

Kantcentrum (Lace Centre) is beside Jeruzalemkerk (*see page 119*).

Museum voor Volkskunde (Folk Art Museum)

40 Rolweg. Tel: 050 339911. Open Apr–Sept 0930–1700 daily; rest of year, exc Tue, 0930–1230, 1400–1700. Closed Jan. Admission: £.

At the sign of the Black Cat café (or *estaminet*, as these small eating and drinking places were known), you enter this intriguing little museum of the everyday life of ordinary working people in the past, housed in 300-year-old former almhouses called Schoenmakersrente (literally 'Shoemakers' rents'). In addition to the café, there are interiors of a cottage, confectioners, a workshop and more.

Carmerstraat

Continue along Balstraat and turn right into Carmerstraat. Here at No 85 is the domed **Engels Klooster** (English Convent). *Open 1400–1600, 1630–1730 daily, closed first Sun each month.* Further along at No 174, the handsome 16th and 17th century **Schuttersgilde Sint-Sebastiaan** (St Sebastian Archers' Guildhall). *Tel: 050 331626. Open Mon, Wed, Fri and Sat 1000–1200, 1400–1700. Admission: £.*

Sint-Janshuismolen

Kruisvest. Tel: 050 448711. Open May–Sept 0930–1230, 1315–1700. Admission: £.

The western edge of the Jeruzalemkerk district is the waterway which used to encircle old Bruges. Along here between Sasplein and Kruispoort, remnants of four waterside windmills remain. The finest of them, and the only one open to visitors, stands near the end of Carmerstraat. Built in 1770 by a co-operative of Bruges bakers, St Janshuismolen still grinds grain today, though just for show, and has a little museum inside.

> **"** The difference between Bruges and other cities is that in other cities you look about for the picturesque, while in Bruges, assailed on every side by the picturesque, you look curiously for the unpicturesque. **"**
>
> **Arnold Bennett, 1896**

Begijnhof (Beguinage) and Minnewater

Open Apr–Sept Mon–Fri 0930–1200, 1345–1730, Sun 1045–1200, 1345–1800.
Rest of year opens half an hour later and closes half an hour earlier.

The walk or ride past the museums and shops, along Mariastraat to the waterside walled enclosure of the Beguinage, makes a delightful and memorable 15-minute outing to one of the loveliest parts of Bruges. The walk eventually reaches the canal, where a picturesque old bridge crosses to the modest Beguinage entrance. Within the cloister wall, simple creamy-white gabled cottages and a church surround a spacious square of flowery lawn shaded by tall trees, like some perfect village green. From time to time nuns stride quietly across the tranquil square, often making their way into the church. Though still wearing the beguine's black and white outfit, these are Benedictine nuns – the last beguine died in 1930.

Beguines were ordinary women, not truly nuns, who took up residence in convent-like homes. They made no monastic vows, were quite free and could leave if they wished, but preferred instead to live in contemplative seclusion, devoting themselves to charitable work and the worship of Jesus. They were particularly a feature of Flanders.

Correctly called **The Beguine Convent of the Vine**, the Bruges Begijnhof was founded in 1245 by Margaret of Constantinople, Countess of Flanders. A traditional Begijnhuisje (Beguine's house) near the entrance is open to visitors, and leads out into a small cloister. With attractive and adequate wooden furnishings and a cosy stove, the impression is of a simple and disciplined, but not spartan, existence.

Minnewater

Beyond the Begijnhof, a delightful path continues under lime trees alongside the canal, where white swans glide on the dark **Minnewater** – or **Lake of Love** (*minne* meaning 'love' in Flemish). Once upon a time this was one of Flanders' busiest docks, where the Reie entered the town and the largest ships loaded and unloaded their wares. Later the river was canalised and extended through the town, and the Minnewater became a reservoir designed to keep the town's canal water at a constant level. Today, its pretty banks are a favourite spot for a picnic or a stroll. There's a delightful lockhouse, 600-year-old remnants of the old fortifications, and always the romantic group of swans.

The story is that the Minnewater swans are here on the orders of Emperor Maximilian of Austria, husband and successor of Mary Duchess of Burgundy, to remind the citizens of Bruges 'for all eternity' of their crime in beheading his councillor, Pieter Lanchals. The councillor's name means 'long neck', and his crest bore a swan. Five centuries later, the citizens have perhaps forgotten their misdeed, but the swans survive, and indeed have become the symbol of Bruges. The story, by the way, originated in the 19th century, when Bruges had been rediscovered and was busy romanticising its heritage.

66 *I resolved to journey along with Quiet and Contentment. These two deities have, I believe, taken Flanders under their special protection.* 99

William Beckford, *Dreams, Waking Thoughts and Incidents*, 1783

Damme

7km north of Bruges, accessible by road or canal.

One of the most enjoyable excursions to be made from Bruges is across the flat and peaceful green polder landscape to the former Zwin river port of Damme. Only a half-hour or so away, the little town was once part of Bruges and existed primarily as the town's outer harbour. Wine warehouses lined the quay, and Damme prospered as did the rest of Bruges. It declined, too, with Bruges. As the Zwin silted up and the fortunes of Bruges faded, Damme followed suit and

gradually became an unimportant village. Like Bruges, a long period of poverty and obscurity helped preserve its appearance and attractions.

Rediscovered, it is now a pretty place of restaurants, antique shops and touristy cafés. Several good eating places line the modest main street, **Kerkstraat**. Menus feature local specialities, such as locally-made cheeses and sausages. Beside the pretty, poplar-lined canal, the **De Schellmolen** mill has been restored and is grinding grain once more. *Open for visits in July and Aug, 1000–1230, 1315–1745. Tel: 050 353319.*

Marktplein

The main market square of Damme is enclosed by charming old houses in the gabled style typical of Flanders. The highlight is its lovely Gothic **Stadhuis** (town hall) (*tel: 050 353319; open May–Sept Mon–Fri 0900–1200, 1400–1800; opens an hour later Sat, Sun and hols; rest of year Mon–Fri 0900–1200, 1400–1700; Sat, Sun and hols 1400–1700; admission: £*). Statues of Flemish counts, set in niches, decorate the façade. Another building of the same period is the exceptionally fine double-gabled mansion, Huyse de Grote Sterre, originally the home of a wealthy citizen. Today it contains the **Damme Tourist Information Office** and the **Tijl Uilenspiegelmuseum (Till Eulenspiegel Museum)**. The popular fictitious Till Eulenspiegel, constantly struggling against Emperor Charles V, was created by 19th century Flemish writer Charles de Coster, and the museum displays drawings, books and even stained-glass windows depicting the local hero.

Onze Lieve Vrouwekerk (Church of Our Lady)

Tel: 050 353319. Open Apr–Sept 1000–1200, 1430–1730. Access to tower. Admission: £.

The town's Gothic church, partly demolished in the 17th century, still has excellent woodcarving and a Baroque altarpiece. The 43m-high tower gives a thrilling vista over the countryside with views reaching into Holland. Sometimes even the sea is within sight.

Sint Jans Hospitaal

Tel: 050 358810. Open Apr–Sept 1000–1200, 1400–1800 daily, exc Mon and Fri (opens an hour later on Sun and hols). Rest of year open Sat and Sun only, 1400–1730. Admission: £.

The former hospital of the Middle Ages now serves as a museum. Its collections of Gothic and Renaissance objects, such as glazed pottery and utensils, as well as paintings and furniture and items from the hospital's chapel, give an insight into life at the time.

Getting there

By paddle-steamer, the *Lamme Goedzak*: Daily Apr–Sept only. Journey time 35 min. A return ticket costs much less than paying the single fare twice. *Tel: 0050 353319.*
Bruges-Damme: From Noorweegse kaai, just beyond Sasplein in the northeast of the town centre on the encircling canal. Departs at 1000, 1200, 1400, 1620, 1800.
Damme-Bruges: From 12 Damse Vaart Zuid. Departs at 0915, 1100, 1300, 1500, 1720.
By horsedrawn carriage, taxi, bicycle or car: A minor road runs beside the pretty tree-shaded canal.
By foot: The canal towpath can be followed all the way from Bruges to Damme.

115

Tourist information

Dienst voor Toerisme, Huyse De Grote Sterre, 3 Jacob Van Maerlandstraat, 8340 Damme; tel: 050 353319; fax: 050 361496. Open 16 Mar –15 Oct Mon–Fri 0900–1200, 1400–1800; Sat, Sun and festivals 1000–1200, 1400–1800. Rest of year closes an hour earlier, and closed in mornings at weekends and festivals.

Eating and drinking

't Brugs Beertje

5 Kemelstraat. Tel: 050 339616. Open 1600–0100, closed Wed. £. The beer-lovers' bar, with 300 varieties – and all served in the right glass. Some of the beers are only available here. The atmosphere is warm, traditional and convivial.

Heer Halewijn

10 Walplein. Tel: 050 339261. Open Wed–Sun only, dinner only. ££. Cosy traditional restaurant with open fire, cheeses and good wines.

De Karmeliet

19 Langestraat. Tel: 050 338259. Open Mon–Sat lunch and dinner, Sun lunch. £££. Serving imaginative variations on a Franco-Belgian theme, located in a grand aristocratic mansion, this is arguably the best restaurant in Bruges. The chef, Van Hecke, is considered one of the best in Europe.

De Lokkedize

33 Korte Vulderstraat. Tel: 050 334450. Open 1900–0300, exc Mon (longer hours at weekends). £. Popular noisy café-bar near Langestraat with jazz, low-lighting and a range of snacks.

Siphon

1 Damse Vaart Oost. Tel: 050 620202. Lunch and dinner only, closed Thur and Fri. ££. Popular place specialising in river eels, steaks and Flemish dishes. Book ahead.

De Vlissinghe

2 Blekerstraat. Tel: 050 343737. Open Mon, Thur, Fri 1600–0100, Wed, Sat 1400–0100, Sun 1130–2100. Closed Tue. Atmospheric and picturesque 17th-century interior in a bar (originally founded in 1515) thought to be the oldest in Bruges.

Visit a Brewery

De Gouden Boom

Museum: 10 Verbrand Niuewland. Brewery: 45 Langestraat. Tel: 050 330699. Open Wed–Sun 1400–1800. Admission: £. If you see drinkers having a glass of beer with a slice of lemon, it could be a Tarwebier, the locally-made wheat beer from De Gouden Boom (The Golden Tree) brewery in the Jeruzalemkerk quarter. Their other beer is Brugse Tripel, a strong brew of 9.5% alcohol. The brewery museum and century-old malthouse are open to the public, and the brewery itself is open to groups of 15. You'll see the old beer-making implements, and get a drink at the end.

De Halve Maan

26 Walplein. Tel: 050 332697. Open Apr–Sept 1000–1700; Oct–Mar at 1100 and 1500 only. Guided visit: ££. De Halve Maan (Half Moon) brewery in Walplein is known for its highly fermented Straffe Hendrik beer. After being shown around the brewery, you are offered a drink.

Shopping

A good place to browse and shop is on the 10-minute walk out to the Beguijnhof via Katelijnestraat, Walplein or Noordstraat.

Lace

Several shop windows are full of delicate handmade fine lace (doilies and placemats are affordable and pretty).

Kantcentrum (Lace Centre)

3A Peperstraat. Tel: 050 330072. Open Mon–Fri 1000–1200, 1400–1800, Sat 1000–1200, 1400–1700. Not just a museum or study centre, the Lace Centre is also a good place to buy lace.

Tapostelientje

Baalstraat 11. Open Mon–Sat 0930–1800, Sun 1100–1600. Either buy lace here, or pick up everything you need to make your own.

Fine chocolates and confectionery

Two of the town's top *chocolatiers* are near 't Zand square, near the Bishops' Palace.

Godiva

36 Zuidzandstraat. Open 0900–1230, 1400–1900. Closed Sun. A well-known high-quality chain of Belgian chocolate shops.

Temmerman

63 Noordzandstraat. Open Fri–Sat 1000–1230, 1400–1830, no lunchtime closing. Closed Sun and Mon am. Real traditional confectioners, making their own beautifully crafted chocolates, biscuits, sweets and spice-breads.

Other good buys

L'Heroïne

Zilverpand 5. Open 1000–1830, closed Sun. Chic fashions and accessories; specialising in Belgian designers.

Markets

Vrijdagmarkt (Friday Market)

't Zand. Sat morning. Despite keeping its original name this traditional general market is now held on Saturdays in this square in the west end of the city centre.

Lace

Exquisite white lace is pinned out neatly in window displays, or hangs in luxuriant drapes within shop doorways. Smaller items – placemats, doilies – are affordable; larger pieces may not be! Though sold as souvenirs to the visitors, this is genuine craftsmanship of the very highest quality and longest pedigree.

Bruges, already renowned for cloth and tapestries, first took up the original **needlepoint** lacemaking (where threads are used to form a framework) in imitation of Italian lacemakers. Flemish ingenuity quickly played its customary role, and **bobbin-lace** (in which the lace is made around pins) was invented, probably in Bruges itself.

The town became Europe's centre of bobbin-lace some five centuries ago. Two hundred years later, prosperous and noble families would not consider anything less than Bruges lace to trim their finery. Not just women, but men too wore plenty of lace as a sign of their wealth. Other Flemish towns also made fortunes from bobbin-lace, some developing their own distinctive styles, notably **Mechelen**, which took over as the leading lace-making town. So vast was the expenditure of pounds sterling on Belgian lace that in 1662 the government tried to prevent it coming into Britain.

Lace connoisseurs know Bruges as the centre of **pillow lace**, and its best-known designs are the flower pattern, the rose lace and the extremely fine form known as **witch-stitch**.

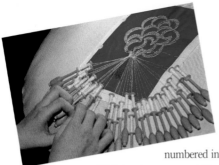

If there seem to be a lot of lacemakers in town today, bear in mind that they once numbered in tens of thousands. The demise of Belgian lace came quickly, and from three causes: new fabrics, new industrial processes and the disappearance of the wealthy class. The 19th century saw the first machine-made lace, and now cheap near-perfect imitations of the handmade styles are readily available. Lace has lost its cachet, and if a Bruges housewife did want to buy some lace today, she would probably choose some that had been imported from the Far East.

Kantcentrum (Lace Centre)

3A Peperstraat. Tel: 050 330072. Open Mon–Fri 1000–1200, 1400–1800, Sat 1000–1200, 1400–1700. Admission: £.

The centre, accommodated in one of Bruges' harmoniously restored almshouses next to the Jeruzalemkerk church, deals comprehensively with the whole subject of Belgian lace. Here you can watch lace being made by experts, the women sitting in rows and moving the bobbins at speed. They are creating fine lace, to both traditional and modern designs. You may speak to them and ask anything you wish about the work – it won't distract them and they are happy to explain. Or you could attend classes here and learn how to do it yourself. In the Centre's museum, the evolution of lace is shown step by step, reaching the ultimate levels of complexity and delicacy in the 18th century.

Brangwynmuseum/ Arentshuis

See page 98.

This town-centre museum of old Bruges has an excellent collection of fine Flemish lace.

Ghent

The greatness of Ghent (Gand in French) has been all but forgotten. This town truly has a sense of both history and continuity, a powerful Flemish medieval city which survived to live in the modern world. Today a busy provincial and university town around a compact historical centre, Ghent enjoys its beer and its food, its energy and enterprise and its memories.

Ghent

Getting there: **By car:** *40 min from Brussels, 20 min from Bruges, on the motorway A10.* **By train:** *30 min from Brussels and Bruges. Hourly departures on most days.*

Touring: **Buses and trams:** *Frequent buses and trams form a comprehensive network covering all areas of town. To get from the station to the town centre, ask for Korenmarkt.* **Carriage trips:** *For a horsedrawn ride around the historic centre of Ghent, pick up a carriage at St Baafsplein. The tours last about 30 min. (Easter–Oct, 1000–1900).* **Boat trips:** *Canal and river tours of Ghent start from Graslei and Korenlei. Some stay within town, others travel to outlying sights. For information call Rederij Benelux, tel: 224 3233, or Gent-Watertoerist, tel: 282 9248, or Bootjes van Gent, tel: 223 8853.*

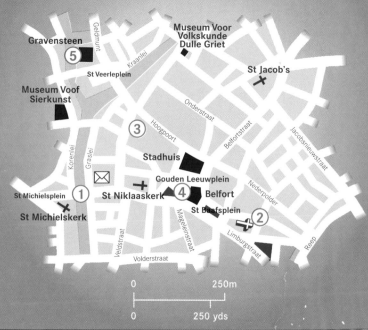

① St Michielsbrug (St Michael's Bridge)

Stand on St Michael's Bridge over the River Leie in the heart of the town and take in the most dramatic overview of the magnificent Graslei and Korenlei quaysides and the pale grey and white Gothic towers rising above historic Ghent. **Page 129**

② Adore the Mystic Lamb

After a chequered history, the astonishingly complex and detailed work by Jan Van Eyck is displayed in a specially protected chapel in the cathedral. You may have to queue to see it, but this painting is one of the treasures of Ghent. **Pages 126–127**

③ Stroll at night

Right through from April to October the great buildings and typical Flemish façades of the old town centre are illuminated at night: the lofty towers and gables bright against the dark sky cast a magical spell under which locals and visitors willingly fall.

④ Go to market

The compact city centre of Ghent is full of squares, large and small, usually one-time markets. Apart from the majestic Botermarkt, there are markets for anything, every day of the week! **Pages 124–125, 133**

⑤ Castle

Ghent's 800-year-old waterside Gravensteen fortress is Belgium's only medieval castle, and is a major attraction. In marked contrast with the elaborately, elegantly decorative Italianate Flemish mansions and palaces of later centuries, the castle reeks of might, power . . . and melodrama. **Pages 128–129**

Gentse Feesten

For ten days, including the week of 21 July, Ghent holds its annual summer carnival, a wild and weird medieval street festival of music, drama, banquets and processions. The town crier announces the start of the celebrations, which are focused on St Jacobs (next to Vrijdagmarkt) but extend all over the city centre.

1500–2000

On 24 February 1500, Ghent's church bells rang out and cannons roared to announce the birth of Charles V, soon to inherit an empire stretching from Flanders to Spain, from the North Sea to Austria, and even across the sea to include territories claimed in the newly colonised Americas. Charles did not see eye to eye with his birthplace, and tried to crush the impudent, rebellious spirit of its wealthy merchants. Today, though, Ghent is proud of its greatest son, and refers to him constantly. In particular, the 500th anniversary of Charles' birth is a focal point for the town's Millenium celebrations.

123

Tourist information

The town's tourist office is in the crypt of the Belfry. *Infokantoor Stad Gent, Raadskeller Belfort, 17A Botermarkt. Tel: 09 266 5232; fax: 09 224 1555. Open daily 0930–1630.*

Botermarkt

Belfort en Lakenhalle (Belfry and Cloth Market)

Botermarkt. Open daily 1000–1230, 1400–1730. Free guided visits in Summer. Admission: £.

> **"** *I can hardly endure to call a place so dignified by such a name.* **"**
>
> **Dorothy Wordsworth, on seeing the Buttermarket in Ghent, 1820**

In Ghent as in Bruges, the covered Cloth Market, which created so much of the wealth of the town, is overlooked by an immense Belfry symbolising the power of trade and the craft guilds. Standing 95m tall in total, with a gilded dragon at its peak, the Belfry has a lift which shoots up to a viewing level 65m high, giving a wonderful view over the town's gabled roofs, streets, squares and riversides. The 52 bells of the carillon can be seen, and there's a bell museum. The Cloth Market itself is undergoing lengthy restorations and is not open to the public.

At the foot of the Belfry stands a bell known as **De Triomfante (The Triumphant)**. The doorway of the old prison at the back of the Belfry is decorated with a strange figure of a *mammelokker*, an adult man suckling milk from a woman. Stranger still to learn than the woman is his daughter, and that this is the legend of Cimon, a Roman Christian condemend to die of hunger but kept alive in this way.

Stadhuis (Town Hall)

Botermarket. Tel: 224 1555 or 233 0772. 40-minute guided tour in English Apr–Sept, Mon–Thur at 1600. Admission: £.

Bringing together Flemish architecture of Gothic (right side) and Renaissance (left side) ages, the Town Hall also brought together Protestant and Catholic when the Pacification of Ghent treaty was signed here in 1576, and read out from the balcony.

The Renaissance section is called **Perchons' House**. The highly decorative Gothic side, with corner turret, the balcony and open staircase, is called the **Keure House**. The mixture of styles reflects the long passage of time that passed between the start of building work and its eventual completion. Such were the city's pretensions at first that it was intended, and assumed, that Ghent's Town Hall would be the largest in Europe. Religious conflicts interrupted the work, which was halted for 60 years and then proceeded with such slowness that a whole new architectural style had been born. The city's pride had declined, too, and the completed Stadhuis, though impressive, was far from being the largest in Europe.

Sint-Niklaaskerk (St Nicholas Church)

Cataloniestraat. Open daily 1000–1700.

The 13th-century church in the main square is Belgium's finest example of the distinctive Schelde Gothic style. Its high spire is one the Three Towers of Ghent which dominate the city-centre skyline.

Vrijdagmarkt and other markets

Apart from the grandeur of Botermarkt, with its magnificent architectural inheritance, Ghent is a town of market squares. Many are still in use. A few paces downstream beyond Graslei, the **Groentenmarkt** (vegetable market) and more historic **Groot Vleeshuis** (meat market) stand by the water. Further downstream (you have to turn away from the river to reach it), a 15th-century cast-iron cannon called **Dulle Griet** stands on the bank close to the large **Vrijdagmarkt**. This 'Friday Marketplace' is a huge square surrounded by impressive Flemish-style brick buildings. Former guildhouses, many are now cafés. In contrast to the aura of power at Botermarkt, the lowlier Vrijdagmarkt long served as a more proletarian main square where, over the centuries, local working people have come not just to buy and sell, but to fight, to celebrate or to be addressed by their rulers.

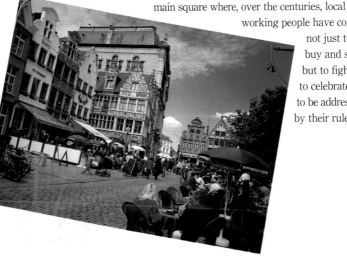

St Baafskathedraal (St Bavo's Cathedral)

Sint-Baafsplein. Open daily 0830–1800. Closed during services (except to attend). Free.

Behind the Belfry lies a large, quiet square in front of Ghent's imposing Gothic cathedral. When St Amand arrived in Ghent in the 7th century, the town was still pagan – mainland Europe was already Christian by this time. Amand founded a monastery and tried to persuade the people to take up Christianity, but their response was to throw him in the River Sheldt. However, Ghent did eventually adopt Europe's new religion, and an abbey built in the 12th century became the focal point of the growing town. It was later to become St Bavo's (or St Bavon's) Cathedral.

Contructed over the course of centuries, the cathedral started in the Romanesque period, and the crypt with its frescoes dates from that time. It continued in a hotch-potch of different, evolving Gothic styles, yet the result is surprisingly harmonious and pleasing. Its **handsome tower** is one of the great landmarks of the city, and gives a glorious view over the historic centre. A tall building with a brick vaulted ceiling, the cathedral **interior** contains a large amount of high-quality craftsmanship, fine doors, an amazing rococo oak and marble **pulpit**, and many priceless **works of art**, including Rubens' *Entry of St Bavo into the Monastery*. Foremost of the artworks is *The Adoration of the Mystic Lamb*, probably by Jan Van Eyck.

The Adoration of the Mystic Lamb

In a chapel to the left upon entering the Cathedral. Open Apr–Oct Mon–Sat 0930–1200, 1400–1800; Sun 1300–1800; Nov–Mar Mon–Sat 1030–1200, 1430–1600, Sun 1400–1700. Admission: £.

The *Mystic Lamb* is a polyptych (i.e. several different paintings on separate panels, comprising a single work) in ten parts depicting as its central idea Christ as an enthroned

High Priest above Christ as a lamb on an altar. It tells the story in sequence of the Christian idea of a progression from the Fall of Man to the Redemption. The immediate impression is of a brilliantly clear, intricately detailed and extremely complex work, of rich and beautiful colours and a wonderful impression of light radiating from the right-hand side. In all there are 248 figures, their expressions poignant and lifelike, in settings of painstakingly accurate textures, fabrics, and vistas and landscapes.

The picture has had a few adventures. The Protestants wanted to destroy it in 1566 but it was protected from them; Emperor Joseph II had the panels of **Adam and Eve** removed because of their nakedness; and the post-Revolutionary Directoire ordered that the work be kept in Paris, where it was dismantled – some of the panels subsequently turned

up at an art museum in Germany. Reassembled in 1920, the bottom left panel, of **The Righteous Judges**, was stolen in 1934: it has since been replaced by a copy. Sent again to Paris for safekeeping at the start of World War II, it was taken by the Germans to a collector in Austria. It was rediscovered by US troops in an Austrian salt mine. Back in St Bavo's Cathedral, since 1986 it has been displayed in a specially protected chapel.

“ *So prodigiously good was the eating and drinking on board these sluggish but most comfortable vessels, that there are legends of an English traveller, who, coming to Belgium for a week, and travelling in one of these boats, was so delighted with the fare that he went backwards and forwards from Ghent to Bruges perpetually until the railways were invented, when he drowned himself on the last trip.* ”
William Thackeray, on travelling by canal in Belgium, 1848

GHENT

Waterside Ghent

The best of old Ghent is alongside the rivers and canals. The town is full of water. Some waterways, like the Muinkshelde, which used to flow behind the Cathedral, have been covered and built over. But much flows openly through the town, the Schelde, Handelsdok, the Lieve, and, curving around the city centre, the Leie, edged by history.

Gravensteen (The Castle)

Tel: 223 9922. Open 0900–1715 (Oct–Mar closes at 1615). Admission: £.

Standing where the Lieve meets the Leie, and surrounded by water, the massive bulk of Ghent's waterside **Castle of the Counts** is the town's most obvious point of interest. Built in the 12th century, it has nothing in common with the elegant mansions and opulent palaces of later centuries. This is the only defensive medieval fortress in Flanders, constructed by the Counts of Flanders to impose their might on the region. It reeks of cruel memories, and contained a notorious underground prison, sometimes partly submerged in water, scene of much inhuman suffering.

Much of what can be seen today is restoration. With its dark stone, its gloomy staircases and turrets, it is sheer theatre: one of the 'attractions' inside is a sickly collection of authentic instruments of torture and execution. Among them a vile-looking red guillotine still has its bag into which the severed head fell (arguably unsuitable viewing for children, though many are brought here). Put all that aside and stand in the open air on the top of the keep. From here the view of Ghent is astonishing, a dream-like vision of the medieval city.

The Patershol district next to the Castle, though still slummy in parts, has also been much restored in recent years and is becoming almost chic, with several good restaurants. Just below the castle walls, old houses enclose St Veerleplein, where once public executions were carried out. Also in this riverside square, the Wennemaershospitaal hospice has a 16th-century façade, and the Oude Vismarkt is a splendid piece of Baroque design and decoration. Following the Leie downstream, the Kraanlei quayside has some striking old houses, and a former children's hospital now containing the Museum voor Volkskunde (Folk Art Museum; *see page 131*).

Korenlei and Graslei

On the left bank of the Leie, upriver from the Lève and at the foot of St Michielsbrug (St Michael's Bridge), the elegant Korenlei is most remarkable for its view of the quayside opposite, Graslei, a stunning ensemble of stepped gables and extraordinarily fine façades. These buildings were a mix of warehouses, storehouses, guildhalls, offices and private homes, and despite a beautiful similarity of style they date from across the centuries, ranging from the 12th century to the 17th.

St Michielsbrug (St Michael's Bridge)

Crossing the Leie between Korenlei and Graslei, this monumental bridge, still busy with traffic, gives an unparalleled view over the grandiose Flemish architecture of the old heart of town. Ahead rise the 'Three Towers of Ghent' – St Nicholas, the Belfry and St Bavo's. Turn to face north (downriver) from the side of the bridge: below are spread the quaysides, with the evocative Gravensteen fortifications rising above the waterside buildings.

The Major Museums

Klein Begijnhof (Small Beguine House)

Violettenstraat. No phone. Open to visitors, but no formal visiting hours. Ask tourist office for latest details.

Hardly a museum, perhaps, since the Beguine building is still in use and a few nuns live here. Founded nearly eight centuries ago, it was restored and reworked at various times, but has not been changed at all during the last 300 years. It has the simple whitewashed brick cottages and appealing calm gardens typical of the Belgian Beguine convents. There was a larger Beguine House near St Elizabeth's Church at pretty little Provenierstraat, founded at the same time but abandoned in the 19th century. Another charming, less ancient Beguine convent survives, with nuns still in residence, out of town at St Amandsberg.

Museum voor Schone Kunsten (Fine Art Museum)

3 Nicolaas de Liemaeckereplein. Tel: 222 1703. Open 0930–1700; closed Mon. Admission: £.

See two amazing works by Hieronymus Bosch – *The Bearing of the Cross*, with its bizarre caricature-like figures, deserves a visit all by itself – and explore the Flemish masters, including Van der Weyden and Frans Pourbus, in this distinguished collection of European art from the 14th century to the middle of the 20th century.

Museum voor Hedendaagse Kunst (Contemporary Art Museum)

Citadelpark. Tel: 221 1703. Open 0930–1700; closed Mon. Admission: £.

Located in the Citadelpark south of the town centre, alongside the Fine Art Museum, this collection continues the story in stark, minimalist settings with exhilarating post-war Belgian and international collections, including Bacon, Magritte, Warhol, Nauman and members of the COBRA group (ie COpenhagen, BRussels, Amsterdam). There are frequent world-class temporary exhibitions.

Museum voor Sierkunst en Vormgeving (Museum of Decorative Arts and Design)

5 Jan Breydelstraat. Tel: 225 6676. Open 0930–1700; closed Mon. Admission: £.

The latest addition to this important museum of furnished interiors is a wing devoted to Art Nouveau and Art Deco. Other sections cover the development of interior décor from Renaissance times to the 19th century.

Museum voor Volkskunde

65 Kraanlei. Tel: 223 1336. Open 1000–1230, 1330–1700; closed Mon. Admission: £.

Located in 18 simple, well-preserved red and white medieval Flemish cottages on the Kraanlei quay, this endearing museum of popular culture is 'set' in about 1900 and deals vividly with the arts and crafts of that time. There is also a puppet theatre here.

Oudheidkundig Museum van de Bijloke (Bijloke Archaeological Museum)

2 Godshuizenlaan. Tel: 225 1106. Individual visits Thur 1000–1300, 1400–1800 and Sun 1400–1800. Admission: £. Groups may visit on any day with advance notice.

The former Bijloke Cistercian monastery, subsequently an abbey, contains a rich collection of very diverse archaeological and historic objects concerning the town's site and the way of life led here. First founded in the 13th century, the brick abbey buildings include some beautifully preserved rooms reworked to reflect historic domestic interiors, while the cloisters exhibit fascinating collections of decorative ceramic and metal domestic art objects. The building is also a principal concert venue for the town.

Schoolmuseum Michel Thiery (Michel Thiery School Museum)

14 St Pietersplein. Tel: 244 7373. Open 0900–1215, 1330–1715; closed Fri pm and Sun. Admission: £.

A complex and comprehensive natural history museum in which a variety of subjects are 'taught' in a schoolroom situation. A scale model shows how Ghent looked at the time of Emperor Charles V, who was born in the town.

Eating and drinking

The main eating, drinking and entertainment areas are Zuidkwarter (South Quarter), the heart of the town from Groentenmarkt to St Baafsplein, the atmospheric Patershol district and the cheaper, student-oriented area around St Pietersplein and Overpoortstraat.

Cafés and bars

Damberg Jazzcafé

19 Korenmarkt. Tel: 225 8433. Open every evening. £. Jazz and drinks, with live open-air performances every Tuesday.

Dreupelkot

Groentenmarkt. Open nightly till 0400 or later. £. Small, cosy and atmospheric setting beside the river for a bar specialising in *genivhre*, Belgium's original gin.

Foley's Irish Pub

10 Recolettenlei. Tel: 225 9085. Open nightly. £. Several nights a week there's live music at this popular bar, sometimes Irish, sometimes Belgian, sometimes from other countries.

Hotsy Totsy

24 Penitentstraat. Tel: 234 0708. Open nightly. ££. Popular upmarket jazz bar with a clubby atmosphere.

Lazy River Jazzclub

5 Stadhuissteeg. Tel: 222 2302. Open nightly. ££. Bar with music, and every Fri 1500–2000 enjoy live jazz on board a river cruise on the Leie.

Restaurants

Brasserie Moka

46 Koerstraat. Tel: 09 225 0054. Open 1100–late evening; closed Sun. ££. Good generous servings of classic Belgian cuisine including Flemish specialities like *waterzooi* and *carbonnade*.

Brooderie

8 Jan Breydelstraat. Tel: 09 225 0623. Open 0800–1800, closed Mon. £. Unpretentious bakery tearoom with tasty meals and snacks at modest prices.

Sint-Jorishof (or Cour St Georges)

2 Botermarkt. Tel: 09 224 2424. Lunch and dinner, closed Sun. ££–£££. This grand and historic mansion in the Buttermarket with its balustraded balcony overlooking the square is now a smart hotel and restaurant. Fine French and Flemish cooking.

Jan Van Den Bon

43 Koning Leopold II Laan. Tel: 09 221 9085. Open for lunch and dinner; closed Sat lunchtime, Sun, festivals, Easter week, mid July–mid Aug, 2 weeks at Christmas. £££. Sit out and enjoy the garden at probably the best restaurant in Ghent, noted for imaginative French cooking.

Shopping

Although not a major shopping town for tourists, Ghent makes shopping easy with its uncrowded pedestrianised town centre and high-quality specialist stores and department stores.

Bygone

12 St Niklaasstraat. Interesting original young women's fashions.

Hot Couture

34 Gouvernementstraat. Classy, relaxed ambience for men's designer clothes.

Oona

12 Bennesteeg. Cool and elegant simplicity here for women's designer fashions.

Siapoo

29 Sluizeken. If you love hats, you'll love this Ria Dewilde hat shop – they can even make hats to order. Some other accessories here too.

Markets

Animals, pigeons, poultry, etc (but no cats or dogs): Oude Beestenmarkt: *Sun: 0700–1300.*
Antiques: Groentenmarkt: *Mon–Thur: 1000–1700.*
Bikes: Oude Beestenmarkt: *Sun 0700–1300.*
Birds: Vrijdagmarkt: *Sun 0700–1300.*
Flea markets: Bij Sint-Jacobs: *Fri 0700–1300;* Beverhoutplein: *Sun 0700–1300.*
Flowers: Woodrow Wilsonplein: *Mon– Sat 0700–1300.* Vrijdagmarkt: *Sun 0700–1300.*
Food: Sint-Michielsplein: *Sun 0700–1300;* Groentenmarkt: *Mon–Sat 0700–1300.*
General markets: Vrijdagmarkt: *Fri 0730–1300, Sat 1100–1800.* Ledebergplein: *Sun 0730–1300.* E Van Beverenplein: *Sun 0730–1300.* Schooldreef: *Mon 0730–1300.*

Clubs, Theatres, Nightlife

Nederlands Toneel Gent

For information and reservations: tel: 09 225 32 08 or consult their website www.ntg.be. Office open Mon–Sat 1100–1700, closed Sun and pub hols. This theatre company plays in three different locations, one of which is KNS, 17 Sint-Baafsplein, which has simultaneous translation into English on Wed, Thur, Fri and Sat at 1930.

De Vlaams Opera (The Flemish Opera)

3 Schouwburgstraat. For information and reservations, tel: 09 225 2425. Website: www.vlaamseopera.be. Ghent's opera house, extensively restored, has a magnificent ceiling and a famously huge chandelier. Productions are of international standard.

Gin

*Although beer and Belgium can be said in a single breath,
there is another, stronger, quintessentially Flemish
Belgian drink. Locals call it* jenever *or* genihvre; *it is
called* genièvre *by the French-speaking population,
rendered into English as Dutch Gin, and better known
simply as gin.*

In fact, this powerful spirit has a score of other names, and there are at least 100 varieties of *genivhre* currently being manufactured in Flanders. It's a long-standing tradition. At least since the 16th century, and perhaps since as long ago as the 14th century, the Flemish have been sipping this distinctive tipple. It's made by blending sprouting barley (about one-third) and rye malt (two-thirds), letting them sweat together at 63°C with some added yeast and fruit (usually juniper berries, but sometimes apple, melon, or other tasty fruit). The whole sugary, alcoholic mix must then be twice distilled to create this powerful malt wine. In

Belgium, it's a drink with real flavour, that packs a punch, and is never served with tonic water or anything else.

By the 1700s, *genivhre* had become widely available and mass produced in Holland, where it was taken up by British sailors. So Flemish *genivhre* travelled across the North Sea and found a willing market in the slums of London's dockland. It soon became known to the English as '**Mother's Ruin**'. Cursed by many, roundly condemned by Church and Government, gin entered England as the cheapest way to drown your sorrows. Laws were passed to control it, taxes were slapped on, and eventually gin became a pricey bourgeois aperitif – except in its native Flanders, where it remains one of the cheapest drinks available in any bar.

135

At least one bar in Ghent specialises in *genivhre*, and doesn't even bother to serve beer: the **Druepelkot**, beside the river at Groentenmarkt.

Lille

Although a major industrial conurbation, the nearest French city to British shores has a large, vivacious and attractive old quarter at its centre. There are impressive remains of its complex frontier history, grand public squares, top quality shopping, and a compelling mix of Flanders and France – in cuisine, architecture, and even in the peculiar patois spoken only here in Lille (Rijssel in Flemish). And there's hardly a tourist in sight.

LILLE

*Getting there: **By train:** Eurostar direct from London Waterloo (journey time 2 hours), Ashford International (1 hour) or Brussels (45 minutes). **By car:** Lille is an hour's drive on autoroute A16/A25 from Channel ferry ports and the Eurotunnel terminal at Calais. It is less than an hour's drive to Brussels on autoroute A27/A8.*

Getting around: Lille's public transport system is a model for other cities. Driverless VAL metro trains come once a minute in rush hours. There is an extensive bus network and a fast modern tramway, the Mongy.

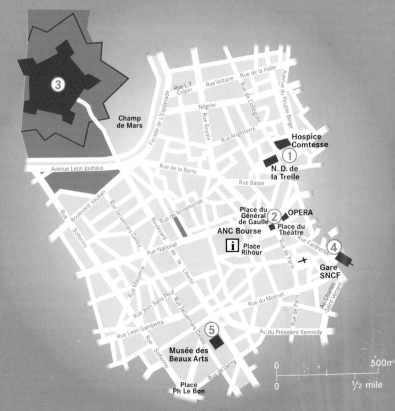

① Vieux Lille

Especially worth seeing are the narrow back streets of Le Vieux Lille, around the medieval Hospice Comtesse. Leading off the squares, this historic quarter is an atmospheric tangle of old cobbled lanes smartened up and lined with chic boutiques and fine food specialists. They lead to the 700-year-old Hospice Comtesse, today an art museum devoted to the Flemish masters.
Pages 144–145

② The main squares

Three grandiose squares – Place Rihour, Place du Théâtre and the huge Place Général de Gaulle (or Grand'Place) – run into each other to create a huge public area of traffic-free relaxation and enjoyment. Here people pause to be entertained by street performers, or sit at café tables beside wildly elaborate Baroque civic buildings laden with gilt and statuary.
Pages 142–143

③ Citadelle

Lille's vast brick citadel, a massive five-pointed star encircled by watery defences, was a vital frontier defence for the new northern border of France after it had annexed the Flemish territory now known as Pas de Calais.
Pages 140–141

④ Euralille Quarter

Medieval, Renaissance and Belle Epoque, and now Lille has thrown itself heart and soul into the 21st century with the construction of an imaginative and audacious new quarter around the modern Lille Europe high-speed rail interchange and the Euralille indoor shopping complex. Pages 146–147

⑤ Musée des Beaux-Arts (Fine Art Museum)

This is one of the best collections in France of the Flemish painters of the 17th-century 'golden age'. Other rooms include Italian and Spanish painters, and the Impressionists. This well laid out museum also contains sculpture, altarpieces, coins, archaeology, ceramics and medieval art. Page 143

Tip

Everything of interest to visitors is within walking distance, but find an excuse to catch Lille's metro. The driverless trains – Véhicule Automatique Léger (Automatic Light Vehicle) – are brilliant, state-of-the-art urban transport, stylish, clean and quiet. The stations too are surprising, imaginative designs complemented by modern murals and sculpture.

What's on

Find out what's happening in the city and keep up to date with events, shows, films, etc, get hold of a copy of the weekly magazine Sortir, *available at hotels, bookshops and in the tourist office.*

Tourist information

Lille's city tourist office is just off Grand'Place. *Office du Tourisme de Lille, Palais Rihour, Place Rihour, Lille. Tel: 03 20 21 94 21. Open Mon–Sat 1000–1800; Sun and hols 1000–1200, 1400–1700.* There's also a regional tourist office, which includes information about places to see on the outskirts of the city or in the surrounding countryside: *CDT, 15–17 Rue du Nouveau Siècle, Lille. Tel: 03 20 57 00 61. Open Mon–Sat 1000–1200, 1400–1700.*

Citadelle

A short walk west of the old quarter, across a protective waterway, the Citadel is entered across a drawbridge and through a rather pompous stone gateway called Porte Royale. Inside, around a pentagonal parade ground, there are officers' quarters, a chapel and a historic arsenal, well restored. Despite its strict functionalism, it is all oddly beautiful.

Considered the greatest masterpiece of Louis XIV's brilliant military architect **Vauban**, Lille's vast fortress was a vital frontier defence for the new northern border of France after it had seized the city, along with the Flemish territory now known as the Pas de Calais, in 1667.

Its extraordinarily complex five-pointed citadel structure, backed up by a further five defensive points, encloses the pentagonal central stronghold. It is surrounded by a protective canal, and includes other water channels that can be flooded, as required, to provide additional security.

Two thousand men worked on the **construction**, using 3 million concrete blocks and 60 million bricks. When complete, the Citadel was capable of complete independence, with its own food stores, wells and tradesmen's shops. Originally, Vauban's fortifications included ramparts around Vieux Lille, but these have disappeared.

In modern times, Lille proved not to be so invincible. The town was taken after a three-day assault by the Germans at the start of World War I, and remained in their hands for most of the conflict. In World War II, after an attack again lasting three days, Lille was once more occupied by the Germans, who used the Citadel as their base. Though bombed by the Allies almost continuously from 1940 1944, it somehow survived. The outer moats were routin used by the Germans as a place of execution for local people; there is a memorial to them in Place Daubenton.

To one side of the access path to the Citadel there is a **zoo**, a **play area** and a **public garden**. Opposite the Citadel stands a **memorial** to Charles de Gaulle, who was born not far away at 9 Rue Princesse. The house, which once had his grandfather's lace works attached, has been turned into a small **museum** of memorabilia of de Gaulle and his life.

Guided 2-hour visits on Sun at 1500, May–Oct only. Contact the Tourist Office (tel: 03 20 21 94 21) to reserve a place.

❝ *Lille is a fortress of the first class. Since the extension of the fortifications in 1858, numerous handsome streets and squares have sprung up. Lille is a very important manufacturing place. Its staple commodities are linen and woollen goods, cotton, cl__, and 'Lisle thread'.* ❞
__eker's *Northern France*, 1905

The main squares

Place Général de Gaulle (Grand'Place)

Lille's main square and medieval marketplace, renamed in honour of the city's most famous modern son, is a vast open space edged with bars and fine old mansions and the astonishingly elaborate **Vieille Bourse**, dating from 1652. The building is arranged as a square around an equally lavishly carved and decorated arcaded courtyard, where once trading was done, deals struck and Lille's fortune increased. This walk-through Renaissance gem has become the rather unlikely setting for a little market of tatty secondhand goods and fragrant flowers.

Place Rihour

Adjacent to main Place Général de Gaulle, smaller Place Rihour is dominated by the octagonal brick tower of the former Palais Rihour. Tel: 03 20 21 94 21. Open Mon–Sat 0900–1900, Sun 1000–1200, 1400–1700.

The Gothic private residence of Duke Philippe the Good of Burgundy, most of the building was badly damaged by fire and never fully reoccupied, though it's now home to the city's tourist office. Beside the Palace stands a huge war **memorial**, and to one side 17th-century houses in the hybrid Franco-Flemish style.

Euralille Quarter

Something happened to Lille in the 1980s. A new energy, a rapid modernisation, an outburst of dynamism, and the city had suddenly thrown off its narrow, industrial image.

SNCF (French Railways) are busy making Lille the hub of an international high-speed rail network. Lille Europe is a completely new, and highly modernistic, railway station, constructed so that Eurostar and Thalys travellers from the UK, Belgium, Holland and Germany can make a simple platform change to the TGVs, the 300km/h *trains à grande vitesse* which now run direct to other French cities without passing through Paris.

The whole area around the station is part of a huge development, the new Euralille Quarter. The station, all light and air and glass and metal, was designed by controversial Dutch architect and Euralille's overall planner Rem Koolhaus and reflects the resurgence of rail travel for the new century.

The hospice used to back onto a busy harbour on an arm of the river Deûle. In the 19th century, the river docks went into decline, and in 1936 the Old Quarter's harbour was filled in and replaced with the Avenue du Peuple-Belge.

Hospice Comtesse

Rue de la Monnaie. Tel: 03 20 49 50 90. Open 1000–1230, 1400–1800 daily, exc Tue and national hols.

This historic charity hospital on the edge of the Old Quarter was almost completely rebuilt in the 17th and 18th centuries and is now one of the town's most interesting buildings. Founded in 1237 by Countess Jeanne de Flandres – hence the name – the hospice changed considerably over the centuries. One of the oldest remaining parts is the 15th-century barrel-vaulted **Salle des Malades** (hospital ward), which has a 17th-century chapel at one end, built so that the sick could attend church services without leaving their beds. Many of the other rooms and halls, including the tiled kitchen and the nuns' dormitory, now house a museum of furnishings, chinaware and porcelain, and artwork.

145

The island

The name Lille comes from L'Ile, 'the island', first mentioned in 1066. The town was indeed surrounded by a marshy, watery terrain of the River Deule. Later canalised, the Deule waterways pass west of the town centre, and were used as part of Vauban's defences. The Flemish name, Rijssel, also means Island.

Le Vieux Lille

The narrow cobbled backstreets of this historic little district are lined with tall, often rather grand, old buildings. Many date from the 17th century, because much of the area was put up in the immediate aftermath of the French takeover of the town. The nearby Citadel was being built at the same time, and there must have been a great air of excitement and change in Lille in those days.

It's clear that there was a distinctive Lille style of façade design, combining bricks and stone. Lille's dynamism and industry perhaps dates from that time: certainly architecture became more and more extravagant, reaching its height in Grand'Place and Place du Théâtre. Then there was a downturn in mood. Lille's experience of siege, hunger, occupation and widespread destruction during both the world wars led to a grim era, and most of these handsome exteriors were covered with featureless facing. In the late 1960s and 1970s, it was decided to restore the Old Quarter, with great success.

Especially impressive are Rue de la Monnaie, Rue de la Grande Chaussée and its continuation, Rue des Chats Bossus, leading to Place du Lion d'Or and Place Louise de Bettignies, near the Hospice Comtesse.

Along these streets and their side turnings there are many attractive clothes stores, specialist shops and good restaurants. Look out particularly for the old Maison des Poissonniers at 15 Place du Lion d'Or, the fine arcaded houses in Rue de la Grande Chaussée, and the Baroque home of Gilles de la Boë at 29 Place Louise de Bettignies. Reaching Rue de la Monnaie, notice the decorated exteriors of 3, 5, 9 and 10 on either side of the Hospice Comtesse.

Place du Théâtre

The smallest and loveliest of the three squares, Place du Théâtre is overlooked on one side by the wildly ornate turn-of-the-century **Opéra**, on which ornament and statuary

seem to be literally climbing out of the walls. Beside it, a musical carillon chimes from the belfry on a lovely brick and stone **Nouvelle Bourse**, now housing the Chamber of Commerce – it's not as old as it looks, dating from the same time as the Opéra. On the other side of the square is the rear of the opulent **Vieille Bourse** building, with restaurant tables set on the pavement outside.

Place de la République

Leading away from the three old squares, Rue Neuve leads into the modern centre of the 'real Lille', just south of the old quarter. Lively pedestrianised **Rue de Béthune** attracts crowds to its cafés and cinemas in the evening, and runs into the large **Place de la République**. Filled with ornamental Second Empire architecture, the square contains Lille's famous **Fine Arts Museum**, rated second most important after the Louvre.

Musée des Beaux-Arts (Fine Arts Museum)

Palais des Beaux-Arts, Place de la République. Tel: 03 20 06 78 00. Open Mon 1400–1800, Wed–Sun 1000–1800. Closed Tue.

Serious art lovers come to Lille just to spend days wandering up and down its corridors. One of France's most distinguished provincial museums, the **Beaux-Arts** contains sculpture, altarpieces, coins, archaeology, ceramics and medieval art, but most of the space is devoted to the 17th century. This is considered one of the most outstanding collections in France of the Dutch and Flemish painters of that period. Other rooms include the galleries of Italian and Spanish painters, and the Impressionists.

143

Conceived and initiated under Lille's imaginative socialist mayor Pierre Mauroy, a former prime minister of France, the Euralille project is a showcase for new architecture and design, covering a large formerly run-down swathe of the city centre. Of the area already complete, the dominant landmark is the **Crédit Lyonnais** tower. Designed by Christian de Portzampac, the glass edifice is known to a gritty Lillois populace as 'The Boot' on account of its L-shape. On the other side of the Eurostar station, a second tower, **Tour Lille Europe**, was designed by Claude Vasconi. North of the high-speed station lies **Parc Henri Matisse**, an integral part of the Euralille Quarter. The southern limit of the new quarter is **Lille Grand-Palais**, a huge modern conference and exhibition space close to Place de la République and the city centre.

Shop 'til you drop

The biggest draw for locals is the vast indoor **Centre Euralille** complex, designed by Jean Nouvel. An enormous indoor shopping area with a hypermarket and over 130 other shops, the Centre also contains an arts complex, a cultural centre, a theatre, restaurants, a hotel and even private apartments.

Architecturally, will it work? Projects which set out to be futuristic have a tendency to look dated within a brief space of time – the whole concept of 'futurism' is already passé. Radical departures from tradition often have only short-lived success. For all that, notwithstanding the odd design of 'The Boot', the indoor shopping complex has been a boon to locals, and there's a feeling that Lille's high-speed rail links are just the start of something big.

147

" *We have a firm chance at last to make Lille into a major European metropolis, and that's my aim.* "
Pierre Mauroy, Mayor of Lille, 1992

Eating and drinking

Cafés and bars

For dozens of popular bars and brassseries offering unpretentious eating and drinking at modest prices, including fresh mussels (as popular here as in Belgian Flanders) and a tempting array of Flemish beers, look around the main central squares – Place Rihour, Place du Théâtre and Place Général de Gaulle – as well as along Rue Neuve, pedestrianised Rue de Béthune and Place Béthune. In Le Vieux Lille, try the popular, youthful brasseries in Rue Basse or Place Louise de Bettignies, behind the Hospice Comtesse. Many bars in these streets have music, and are open very late, or until dawn. For example, Le 30 in Rue de Paris, has live jazz nightly after 2100.

Restaurants

For good quality eating look around the Place Rihour, Place du Théâtre, Place Général de Gaulle and Place Béthune. For lower budget, but acceptable, eateries, the area close to Lille-Flandres station is worth exploring. During the day, fast-food snackeries and restaurants can be found inside the Euralille Centre Commercial.

Bar de la Cloche

13 Place du Théâtre. Tel: 03 20 55 35 34. Open all day and until midnight. ££. Amiable wine bar and restaurant in this charming square, reasonable food at all hours, local specialities.

Caveau de Bacchus

196 Boulevard Victor-Hugo. Tel: 03 20 57 35 00. Open approx 0900–2330. ££. Likeable wine-bar and restaurant offering good solid French eating at its heartiest, beef, sausages, stews.

La Galetière

4 Place Louise de Bettignies. £. Good, popular crêperie in busiest part of the Old Quarter.

L'Huîtrière

3 Rue Chats Bossus. Tel: 03 20 55 43 41. Lunch and dinner. Closed Sun pm. £££. Several Lille restaurants have won high acclaim, few more than this beautiful fish restaurant, located in the midst of the Old Quarter.

Le Sébastopol

1 Place de Sébastopol. Tel: 03 20 57 05 05. Lunch and dinner. Closed Sat lunchtime. £££. Art Deco interior, crisp professionalism and high-class classic cooking.

Le Varbet

2 Rue Pas. Tel: 03 20 54 81 40. Lunch and dinner. Closed Sun and Mon. £££. Good little restaurant in the town centre with some unusual dishes, such as excellent blinis.

Shopping

Euralille

Lack-for-nothing indoor shopping can be found at Euralille Centre, a five-minute walk from Place Général de Gaulle. This huge, attractive indoor shopping complex feels like a multi-storey pedestrianised town centre. Everything is here, from fashions to food, kitchenware to kitsch, with heaps of French quality and style.

You'll see Euralille Centre as soon as you arrive, as it's close to the austere Lille-Europe station, where Eurostar arrives. The purpose-built station's light-and-air concept forms an integral part of the overall plan for Lille's major new development, the Euralille Quarter, a showcase for innovative architecture and design.

Vieux Lille

Historic Vieux Lille's atmospheric tangle of narrow cobbled lanes have been smartened up and lined with chic boutiques and fine food specialists. It's a charming, easy place to shop for cheeses, handmade chocolates, fine lace and other French and Flemish specialities.

On the way, linger at top-quality cheese specialist **Christian Leclerq** at 9 Rue Lepelletier – you'll know it by the smell. The shop has its own restaurant with a menu featuring La Tour de France des Fromages Chauds. The superb little baker's, **De La Treille**, is on the corner of Rue Lepelletier and Rue Basse. Lavishly ornate **Pâtisserie Méert**, at 27 Rue Esquermoise, is a heaven of wonderful cakes, waffles and home-made chocolates.

Markets

Place du Concert
Wed, Fri and Sun. General market.

Solférino
Along Rue de Solférino. Wed and Sat. Busy general market.

Vieille Bourse
Inside the inner courtyard of the historic former Bourse. Daily. Flowers and second-hand books.

Wazemmes Market
Near St Pierre and St Paul church, Sun mornings. Colourful market for antiques, fresh seafood and flowers, as well as other food and general market stalls.

Tip

While in Lille, try some of the biscuits – petits beurres *and* gauffres fourrés *– that are a speciality of the city's patisseries and boulangeries. Try too the local French-Flemish confectionery called* Bêtises de Cambrai. *Several unbelievable explanations are offered for the strange name of these minty boiled sweets – Cambrai is a nearby town, and 'Bêtises' is slang for something utterly stupid.*

Giant Festivals

If you're here at the right moment, you'll see one of the strangest customs of Flanders, whether Belgian or French. Huge brilliantly painted models, normally one of a man and one of a woman, though sometimes of a whole family, all dressed in traditional local costume, lead a big procession around town.

Belgium loves festivals and processions. The year is full of them. Often there is a religious theme, but almost as often the festival has a secular origin. And many of these traditional events involve a Giant.

The Giants are made of lightweight materials, generally wickerwork and papier maché, and are pushed around or carried from inside. Literally a figurehead or a model citizen, the Giant represents the people of the town writ large. Half lifelike, half caricature, they often depict real historical personages, and usually form part of a legend about the community.

In some towns, there is a special story or song to accompany the appearance of the Giants, who may be great warriors in armour, ferocious pirates, brave women, valiant defenders, or simple local citizens.

The festival in Lille

One of the earliest and most famous Giant Festivals, and still one of the biggest, is in Lille (3rd Sunday after Whit Sunday), when the city's 17-m-high Giants Lydéric and Phinaert lead the festivities. According to their tale, Phinaert was a terrible highwayman who lived in a great fortress on the spot where Lille stands today. One day Phinaert attacked and robbed the Prince of Dijon and his wife, killing the Prince. His wife escaped, gave birth to a boy and gave him to a hermit-monk who had him suckled by a doe, and named him Lydéric. The young man, reaching manhood, vowed to avenge his parents, challenged Phinaert to a fight, and killed the highwayman. Lydéric then took control of the castle and all the surrounding lands, and made the country safe for habitation.

In later years, Lille adopted more Giants: Jeanne Maillotte, who led the women of the city against robbers in the 14th century, and Gambrinus, the 'King of Beer'.

Other festivals

On the Belgian side of the border, one of the biggest and best Giant Festival is at Ath, west of Brussels on the River Dender (4th Sunday in August). Here Monsieur and Madame Gouyasse, together with the Four Aymon Sons, and even their amazing giant horse Bayard, together with Samson, Ambiorix and Mamzelle Victoire – all representing a wonderful hotch-potch of history, myth and legend – lead a jolly day of celebration.

Excursions

Get out of town – fast. And it is fast in Belgium, a country so small, and so well-served by highways and public transport, it takes only about an hour from Brussels to reach Holland or France, Germany or the North Sea coast. Travel is easy, journeys brief and there's a huge amount to see all over this populous land.

EXCURSIONS

Excursions

Getting there: *Every Belgian railway station provides travel information about the whole network. Information telephone numbers at main stations: Antwerp 03 204 2040; Bruges 050 382 382; Brussels 02 555 2555; Ghent 09 222 4444. Weekend Returns give discounts of 40 per cent for one person, 60 per cent for a second traveller. Other low-cost passes and special reductions are sometimes available. For information on rail travel in Belgium while in the UK, call 0891 516444.*

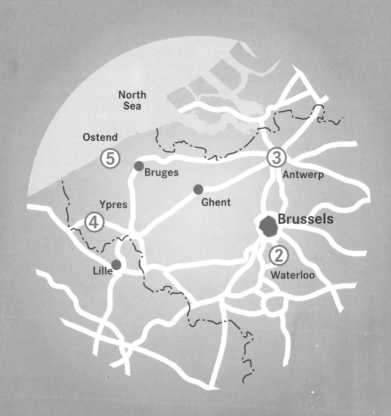

North Sea

Ostend

⑤

Bruges

③

Antwerp

Ypres

Ghent

④

Brussels

②

Lille

Waterloo

① Catch a train

Inexpensive, frequent, clean, punctual, the trains are the best way to make a quick and easy excursion to another part of Belgium. Driving doesn't compare. **Page 154**

② Waterloo

No, it's not just a railway station. History buffs and others won't need to be told that the battle at this spot just outside Brussels in June 1815 put a dramatic end to French ambitions and so changed the whole character of Europe. **Pages 156–157**

③ Antwerp

If you're not short of time, the booming energy and vitality of historic Antwerp deserves as much as you can give. It's a vivacious, artistic, forward-looking city, which also has a wealth of sightseeing and treasures from the past. **Pages 158–159**

④ In Flanders Fields

The fine old Flemish town of Ypres, whose name is so associated with World War I, is far from being a wasted battleground. Immaculately rebuilt, it poignantly recalls those times, while fully enjoying its life today. Don't miss its 'In Flanders Fields' interactive museum.
Pages 164–165

⑤ Ostend

Belgium's principal ferry port is also a smart beach resort, where the well-to-do used to have holiday villas or come for weekends. While that's no longer true, it remains a relatively upmarket area, and a great spot for fish or shellfish at busy quayside restaurants. **Pages 162–163**

Touring by rail

B-Dag trips: Belgian Railways have teamed up with over 100 attractions around the country to offer low inclusive rates for travel and entry fees. Where necessary, a trip by bus, tram or underground is also included. B-Dag+Bike is another appealing excursion formula combining the B-Dag fare with a day's bike hire from the local station. High-quality lightweight tourers and mountain bikes are available at 35 stations, including Ghent, Ypres and Ostend. You can choose between bikes for men and women, and in different sizes, but it's wise to contact the station in advance to make sure the bike of your choice is available.

Rail touring ticket: A 5-day card allows travel throughout Belgium (with the exception of frontier points) within any period of five days you select. It is valid for one month.

Tourist information

Two separate offices are located in the travel information centre at 61 Rue du Marché-aux-Herbes.
OPT (for places in Wallonia/French-speaking Belgium): *tel: 02 504 0200; fax: 02 513 69 50.*
VCGT (for places in Flanders): *tel: 02 504 03 00; fax: 02 513 69 50.*

Waterloo

Autoroute RO sweeps indifferently across the Waterloo plain where the future of Europe was decided one gruesome day in 1815.

It skirts the distinctive 45m-tall grassy pyramid of the **Butte du Lion** memorial, topped by a massive cast-iron lion, erected by the Dutch in 1826 to mark the spot where Prince William of Orange was wounded during the fighting. On the evening of 18 June 1815, the farmland around this spot was covered with 49,000 dead and dying bodies, blood soaking through their smart uniforms, and Napoleon Bonaparte's dream of uniting Europe under French law had been shattered.

To understand what happened here, and why, first call in at the **Visitor Centre** at the foot of the hill. A film explains and re-enacts the battle, and a large model shows where everything took place. A fascinating earlier attempt to educate visitors also survives: the **Grand Panorama**, created in 1912. The circular interior wall of this large rotunda is painted with an immense all-round dramatic scene intended to give some sense of what it was like to be standing in the midst of the battle.

On the N5 south of Plancenoit, the **Caillou Farmhouse**, where Napoleon planned his attack, and where he slept on the eve of battle, has been turned into an interesting small museum. The bedroom has been recreated, and some of the Little Emperor's possessions are displayed. Similarly, in Waterloo, the inn where the Duke of Wellington stayed has become the **Wellington Museum**, with reconstructions, mementoes and a display devoted to the course of the battle.

What happened at Waterloo

In June 1815, the English, Dutch and Prussians, threatened by Napoleon's sweeping imperial vision, joined forces to defeat him. 'L'Empereur' had huge popular support in France, with a vast and enthusiastic army carried forward by a patriotic fervour to 'liberate' Europe, including Britain and Ireland.

His immediate response was to tackle the Prussians separately – he already knew that, on their own, no single foreign army could beat him.

He was proved right on 14 June in his first encounter, trouncing the Prussians at Ligny, near Charleroi. However, Napoleon knew the Prussian force would soon recover – so he set off at once to see off the Duke of Wellington, commanding the English and Dutch forces. On 17 June his tireless army arrived at Waterloo, intending to launch the attack the next morning. Napoleon based himself outside the village of Plancenoit, while Wellington took up a position at Waterloo.

Chaussèe de Waterloo, the old road south from Brussels to Waterloo, is a bustling thoroughfare lined with shops, bars and restaurants, especially around the junction known as La Bascule.

The weather at first light on 18 June was so bad that Napoleon decided to hold off for a few hours, which might help too because more French troops were on their way. In the afternoon, he focused on seizing key landmark farmhouses. After a bloody struggle, inflicting massive losses on both sides, the French moved forward, taking two of the farmhouses and continuing into the so-called Chemin Creux (Sunken Road). Though very much weakened, Wellington's men grabbed the opportunity to damage the French as they crossed this vulnerable low-lying location.

Just then, the rapidly regrouped Prussians arrived, bombarding the French from the rear as they struggled across the Chemin Creux. Attacked from both sides, within a few hours the French were reduced to a tiny group literally running for their lives. Napoleon conceded defeat, and Allied commanders, Wellington and the Prussian von Blucher, met for a celebration dinner at the Belle Alliance tavern near Plancenoit overlooking the battle site.

Tourist Information

Getting there: *20km south of Brussels. Frequent trains from Gare Centrale/Centraalstation.*
Tourist information: *149 Chaussée de Bruxelles. Tel: 02 354 9910.*
Butte du Lion: *252 Route du Lion, Braine l'Alleud. Tel: 02 385 1912. Open Apr–Oct 0930–1830 daily. Rest of year 1030–1600. Admission: £.*
Visitor Centre: *Tel: 02 385 1912. Open Apr–Oct 0930–1830 daily. Rest of year 1030–1600. Admission: ££.*
Grand Panorama: *Tel: 02 384 3139. Open Apr–Oct 0930–1830 daily. Rest of year 1030–1600. Admission: £.*
Caillou Farmhouse: *Tel: 02 348 2424. Closed Mon. Open Apr–Oct 1000–1830 daily. Rest of year 1330–1700. Admission: £.*
Wellington Museum: *Tel: 02 354 7806. Open Apr–mid-Nov 0930–1800 daily. Rest of year 1030–1700. Admission: ££.*

Antwerp

Belgium's great undiscovered city, Antwerp looks and feels like a treasure chest, filled to the brim with valuables, ancient and modern. Formerly one of the great trading cities of Europe, and still one of the world's largest ports, it brilliantly combines commerce with culture.

Above all Antwerp is associated with art. The 1999 extravaganza celebrating the 400th anniversary of Antwerp master Anthony van Dyck has obscured the fact that this is also the city of Rubens, Jordaens, Bruegel and Plantin. In fact, Van Dyck was Rubens' pupil, and Plantin's family ran a prestigious publishing house for which Rubens provided designs and book illustrations. The work of all of these local artists is abundantly represented in Antwerp's museums (*see pages 160–161*).

The city is also the world's biggest diamond capital, with four diamond exchanges and well over 1000 diamond companies. No fewer than 85 per cent of all the world's rough diamonds are traded in this one town, and 50 per cent of cut diamonds, netting the city tens of billions of dollars annually.

Around Grote Markt

Antwerp's historic centre on the right bank of the Scheldt/Schelde comes as a dazzling surprise. Essential viewing for every first-time visitor should be the wonderful **Grote Markt**, the delightful, colourful unevenly-shaped central market square surrounded by tall 16th- and 17th-century Guildhalls, with gilded façades and Italianate Flemish dècor run riot. Along one side is the long **Stadhuis (Town Hall)** in Renaissance style (*tel: 03 220 8211, Mon, Tue, Wed 0900–1500; Sat 1200–1550. admission: £*), while standing in the square is a fountain depicting Antwerp's most gruesome traditional legend: a severed hand of the giant Druon Antigon, swung aloft by Roman soldier Silvius Brabo. The story supposedly explains the name of the city – which sounds a little like Handwerpen, or 'hand throwing'.

Looming far above the rooftops of Grote Markt, and dominating the old quarter, is the mass and height of Antwerp's extraordinary **Onze-Lieve-Vrouwekathedraal (Cathedral of Our Lady)**. Covering almost a full hectare of land (2.5 acres), the building has seven aisles and is filled with valuable artworks, including several paintings by Rubens. It also has a massive bell tower (123m) of elaborate and delicate open stonework. Inside there's a carillon with 47 bells, which give concerts on Fridays at 1130 and Mondays at 2100.

Just north of the cathedral, don't miss the **Oude Beurs**, the former commodities exchange almost five centuries old, and close by, the **Vleeshuis**, the fantasy Gothic guildhall of Antwerp's butchers, built in 1501, the façade in red and white stripes and topped with turrets. Inside, it houses a collection of rare harpsichords.

The grim fortress on the riverside is the **Steen**, built 1100 years ago to guard the city when it was a new settlement, now Antwerp's **Maritime Museum** (*open 1000–1700 daily, exc Mon; admission: £*).

Boat trips

Boat tours of the huge, busy harbour (Havenrondvaart) are top favourite, and the sight of the multitude of ships, warehouses and heavy industrial complexes is awesome and inspiring. River excursions along the industrialised Scheldt (Scheldetocht) give a magnificent perspective on the historic city centre. The trips, run by the Flandria Shipping Company, leave from the Steen quayside (*tel: 03 231 3100*) in the city centre.

Getting there: *Antwerp is about 44km north of Brussels on motorway A1 (E19). Frequent trains from Brussels Midi Station, 40-50 min.*

Antwerp's major art museums

Antwerp has a score of great museums, and its art collections are prodigious. Here are some of the best.

Koninklijk Museum voor Schone Kunsten (Royal Museum of Fine Art)

1–9 Leopold de Waelplaats. Tel: 03 238 7809. Open 1000–1700 daily, exc Mon. Admission: £, free on Fri. This immense collection of Belgian art traces the history of Flemish painting from the Primitives to the Surrealists and beyond, with representative pieces by most of the leading artists in each period. The Ground Floor is devoted to Modern Art, the First Floor to the Old Masters.

Mayer van den Bergh Museum

Lange Gasthuisstraat. Tel: 03 232 4237. Open 1000–1700 daily, exc Mon. Admission: £. The former private collection of world famous art collector Fritz Mayer van den Bergh, mainly of medieval paintings, manuscripts, tapestry and sculpture.

MUHKA (Museum voor Hedendaagsekunst) (Museum of Contemporary Art)

16–30 Leuvenstraat. Tel: 03 238 5960. Open 1000–1700 daily, exc Mon. Admission: £. In an Art Deco former grain warehouse near the river, south of the city centre, this resolutely modern art museum exhibits the latest trends, with an emphasis on Belgian work.

Museum voor Fotografie (Photography Museum)

47 Waalse Kaai. Tel: 03 216 2211. Open 1000–1645 daily, exc Mon. Free. The whole history of photography explained, together with a wonderful collection of works by most of the great names, including Man Ray, Cartier-Bresson, Brassaï, Irving Penn and others.

Openluchtmuseum voor Beeldhouwkunst (Open-Air Sculpture Museum)

Middleheimlaan. Tel: 03 828 1350. Open daily, exc Mon. 1000; closes at 1700 Oct–Mar, 1900 in Apr and Sept, 2000 in May and Aug, 2100 in June and July. Free. Located in the spacious greenery of Middleheim Park, this unusual museum displays more than 300 sculptures in the open. Works representing every period from Rodin to the present are displayed.

Plantin-Moretus Museum

22 Vrijdagmarkt. Tel: 03 233 029. Open 1000–1645 daily, exc Mon. Admission: £. Christopher Plantin was a prosperous printer of the 16th century, noted for high-quality work and for his own high culture and learning. Friend of the wealthy and powerful, including the monarch, he founded a great dynastic family noted for their love of art. The art museum in this former home and printworks of the family displays a rich and varied collection of rare artworks, books and manuscripts.

Rockoxhuis (Rockox House)

Keizerstraat. Tel: 03 231 4710. Open 1000–1700 daily, exc Mon. Admission: £. The private collection of 17th-century Antwerp burgomaster Nikolas Rockox, displayed in his fascinating restored home, includes an eclectic array of works by Rubens, Joradens and Van Dyck.

Rubenshuis (Rubens House)

9 Wapper. Tel: 03 232 4747. Open 1000–1645 daily, exc Mon. Admission: £. Although the paintings of Pieter Paul Rubens can be seen in numerous museums and churches of Belgium, it is intriguing to visit the 16th-century master's home in the centre of Antwerp. It has been immaculately restored and even the garden is believed to be exactly as it was in his day.

Getting there: Frequent non-stop trains from Brussels Midi Eurostar station to Antwerpen Centraal station. Journey time 40-50 min. Be sure to ask for Antwerpen Centraal and not one of the city's other stations.

Getting around: Antwerp has an efficient little metro system, together with an extensive network of buses and trams operated by De Lijn. For a single ticket ask for a 'direct/direkt'. For better value, buy a *carnet* of 10. Or a Day Ticket may be the right choice, available on the vehicles or in De Lijn shops. Further information: *De Lijn, 58 Grotehondstraat; tel: 03 218 1406.*

Tourist information: City information office: *15 Grote Markt, Antwerp. Tel: 03 232 0103. Open 0900–1800 Mon–Sat, 0900–1700, Sun.*

Regional information office: *11 Karel Oomstraat. Tel: 03 216 2810. Open 0900–1800 Mon–Sat, 0900–1700, Sun.*

Ostend and the Coast

There's much more to Ostend than its busy ferry port. This classy little resort has a good beach, a casino and quality shopping. Visserskaai (Fishing Quay) is the colourful quayside where fresh fish and shellfish are bought and sold and served up in lively restaurants – they're famed for oysters. Behind the quays are the narrow streets of the Fishermen's Quarter.

Kapellestraat, Ostend's main shopping street area, runs from central square Wapenplein to the yacht marina, and some of its side turns and neighbouring streets. Along here familiar fashion chains rub shoulders with large and small specialist stores selling handmade chocolates, Belgian designer clothes, traditional lace and souvenirs.

The **Museum voor Schone Kunsten (Fine Art Museum)** (*Wapenplein, Feest-en-Kultuurpalleis; tel: 059 805335; open 1000–1200, 1400–1700 daily, exc Tue; admission: £*) gives pride of place to James Ensor, the half-English Ostend artist whose strange paintings are classed as precursors of Surrealism. **James Ensorhuis (James Ensor's home)** (*27 Vlaanderenstraat; tel: 059 805335; open June–Sept and during Christmas and Easter hols 1000–1200, 1400–1700; admission: £*) has also been restored and turned into a museum. His studio is on the second floor, above his parents' seashell and souvenir shop. The **Museum voor Moderne Kunst (Museum of Modern Art)** (*11 Romestraat; tel: 059 508118; open 1000–1800 daily, exc Tue*)

displays Ostend's excellent collection of 20th-century art, including Expressionism, Abstract art and Pop Art.

Ostend's busy **Kursaal (Casino)** is considered more as a cultural centre than gaming rooms. It contains a theatre, art exhibitions and a concert hall, which von Karajan extravagantly declared had 'the best acoustics in the world'. The Casino is also the central venue for festivals and events like the curious annual Dead Rat Fair (*first Saturday in March*), when men dress as masked women.

The **Kusttram (Coast Tram)** runs up and down the 70km Belgian coast all day long, taking just 2 hours for the journey, most of the distance alongside the beach. You can get on and off at will, pausing at resorts on the way. Key places worth visiting: **Knokke-Heist** (say it 'Kuh nock kuh'), now Belgium's most upmarket resort, with 50 art galleries, a casino and a whole string of jewellery stores; **De Haan**, still full of Belle Epoque style; and **De Panne**, where sand-yachts catch the breeze on an immense beach, while nearby nature reserve De Westhoeck is a haven for sand-loving wildlife.

Getting there: *Frequent trains from Brussels Midi station to Oostende, journey time about an hour and 10 minutes.*
Tourist information: *Toerisme Oostende, 2 Monacoplein. Tel: 059 701199. Mon–Fri 0900–1700.*

Besieged

When the Siege of Ostend started in 1601, Archduchess Isabella did not expect it to last long. She laughingly said she would not change her underwear until it was over. The Siege lasted three years, 70,000 people died, and the word Isabella entered Ostend speech, to describe a murky, worn-out colour.

Ieper (Ypres)

The glorious 1000-year-old Gothic cloth-making town known to British 'Tommies' in World War I as 'Wipers' was almost entirely demolished during that heartless conflict. It had once been one of the three great centres of medieval Flemish culture (alongside Bruges and Ghent). Yet, such was its power of endurance, that Ypres was painstakingly and perfectly reconstructed.

The town vowed never to forget the horror of that war, and has remained true to that promise. At its Menin Gate, the names of nearly 55,000 British soldiers are recorded, and here the Last Post is sounded every evening at 2000.

The grandest building in Ypres, very symbol of its wealth, is the huge central Lakenhalle, or Cloth Halls, a magnificent Gothic extravaganza dating from 1304. It stretches most of the way across the enormous Grote Markt (main market square), in the heart of town, where there is still a big street market every Saturday. The Lakenhalle's lovely square Belfort (belfry), gives a wonderful view over the town – if you don't mind climbing 264 steps. Inside, there is a carillon of 49 bells, which play concerts on Sunday evenings in summer (*2100–2200*). The Lakenhalle houses the In Flanders Fields Museum.

In Flanders Fields Museum

Lakenhalle, 34 Grote Markt. Tel: 057 228584. Open Apr–Sept 1000–1800 daily; Oct–Mar Tue–Sun 1000–1700. No entry to museum less than an hour before closing time. Admission: ££.

This dramatic and educational museum takes you on a walk through time, following the progress of World War I through the eyes of ordinary people as historic Ypres is turned into a battlefield.

The First Battle of Ypres in November 1914 was the start of a major German offensive: the shelling of the city began. The Second Battle of Ypres in April–May 1915 completed the destruction of the town; poison gas was used against soldiers for the first time. The Third Battle of Ypres took place in 1917, with three months of continuous fighting at the site. The Final Offensives of 1918 repelled a last-ditch effort by the Germans. When the Armistice was signed later that year, half a million foreign soldiers lay dead at Ypres.

The Museum's innovative approach is to allocate a real person from that time to each visitor, and accompany them as they live through the years 1914–18. As well as dioramas, film, interactive multimedia displays and effects, there are authentic personal belongings and genuine historical detail. The effect can be emotional.

Swing a cat

Every three years on the second Sunday in May, Ypres celebrates with its bizarre **Cats' Festival**. Stuffed toy cats are thrown from the Belfry while a procession of cat-masked 'witches' parades below. Once upon a time, the cats were real, and were associated in the local mind with evil and magic. Nowadays, the festival has become a real carnival with a Giant Cat, plus 2000 actors, floats, horses, processions and entertainment, all on a catty theme. The next festival is in the year 2000.

Getting there: *By road, 25km from Lille, 76km from Ghent, 120km from Brussels. Frequent trains to Ieper from Brussels Midi station, journey time 1hour 35min, and from Brugge (change at Kortrijk), journey time 1hour 30min.*

Tourist information: *Sted. Dienst voor Toerisme Ieper, 34 Grote Markt. Tel: 057 200724. Open Mon–Sat 0900–1800, Sun 1000–1800; Oct–Mar closes an hour earlier.*

Lifestyles

Shopping, eating, children and nightlife

167

Shopping

Shopping in Brussels, Bruges and the rest of Belgium is about luxury and high quality. The country has respected traditional skills dating back to the great days of Flemish craftsmanship. Although Belgium has hypermarkets and ordinary shops for everyday purchases, it is in small specialist stores that the best of shopping is to be found.

Lace and chocolates and diamonds, for example, are pure Belgium – and while these goods are relatively inexpensive here, they are not for budget shoppers. And even though Belgium makes hundreds of quality traditional beers, they appeal to connoisseurs rather than the 'booze run' bargain hunters.

There's another side to Belgian shopping. The country's dynamic world of fashion design has won worldwide attention. In jewellery too there's a new Belgian style worth looking out for.

Shopping in Lille, which has the same history, preoccupations and skills as other Flemish towns, is similar, but with the added dimension of low-priced high-quality French foods, wines, kitchenware and household goods.

Souvenirs

Tacky and tasteless, but fun (maybe), are the ubiquitous models of Tintin and Mannekin Pis. Tintin especially has been comprehensively merchandised, so T-shirts, souvenirs and toys of Tintin and Snowy are must-buys for families with young fans. There's even a whole shop devoted to 'the boy reporter' at **La Boutique de Tintin** (*13 Rue de la Colline*). The horrible Mannekin Pis comes as mini version, full size garden gnome, and everything in between, including bottle opener (the corkscrew being … yes, that's right). Most of the best, or worst, are to be found in souvenir shops close to the wee man himself.

Better quality and more worthwhile are small lace pieces, imitation tapestries, packaged handmade chocolates, and souvenir boxes of Belgian beer, available at hundreds of stores in the city centre.

Antiques

High-class antiques are a popular purchase with both locals and visitors. So is cheaper, but quirky and interesting, *brocante* – secondhand goods. In Brussels, both lie alongside each other in the Sablon and Marolles districts. The two Sablon squares and surrounding streets are edged with expensive antique shops, while Grand Sablon square itself is filled by dealers selling an eclectic mix of secondhand pictures, ornaments and furniture.

At the foot of the Sablon, the working-class Marolles quarter has similar shops, but specialising in less expensive goods. In Marolles' daily flea market it may often be possible to find real quality hidden among the assorted bric-à-brac. As well as antiques, many buyers are keen to find decorative 1950s and 1960s paraphernalia, as well as more valuable wartime relics and older Art Nouveau pieces.

Many Brussels shops have narrow specialities, concentrating on, for example, secondhand oriental rugs (Ghadami, *1 Rue des Minimes*), old books (Genicot in Galerie Bortier, *Rue St Jean*), maritime paraphernalia (Historic Marine, *39 Rue du Lombard*), fountain pens (Style & Kezoen, *124 Rue Blaes*), even office equipment (Antik Blaes, *3 Rue Blaes*). Auction houses cover the whole range (Galerie Moderne, *3 Rue du Parnasse*).

Bruges, Ghent, Antwerp and Lille also have secondhand markets and flea markets and antiques fairs.

Lille's annual **Braderie de Lille** is a huge three-day antiques and secondhand fair filling the town centre every year on the first weekend in September.

Beer

Belgian beer is wonderful, and a whole subject worthy of study (*see pages 174–175*), but where to buy some to take home? Souvenir shops have pre-packed selections, but often at high prices. Ordinary grocers and supermarkets are mainly found in residential areas away from the city centres, and the choice can be confusing. Look out for beer specialists for the best range at reasonable prices, such as Bière Artisanale (*174 Chaussée de Wavre, Brussels*) and Woolstreet Company (*31a Woolestraat, Bruges*). Both are helpful and sell many hundreds of varieties of beers, as well as the appropriate glass for each kind.

Cartoons

Belgian cartoon-strip is generally in book form, rather than comic magazines. The commerce in cartoons is not just tourist-driven: Belgians assert that they too love cartoons, and have done so for a hundred years. Several shops around Brussels specialise in cartoon books, mostly written in French, sometimes translated into Flemish, English and other languages. Other bookshops have big cartoon sections, aimed as much (or more) at adults than children. Take a look at Brüsel (*100 Boulevard Anspach*), for a wide

selection. Another good source is the bookshop at the Centre Belgie de la Bande Dessinée (Cartoon-Strip Centre) (*see page 53*).

Chocolates and confectionery

The famous Belgian chains, such as Leonidas, Godiva and Neuhaus, sell high-quality chocolates at reasonable prices and have branches all over the country and abroad. Alternatively, visit individual *chocolatiers* where the quality can be even higher. These you'll find in every town centre, but may have to seek local advice to find out who is the very best! Two well-known Brussels names are Pierre Marcolini *(39 Place du Grand Sablon)*, considered among the best of Belgium's *chocolatiers*, and Wittamer (*12–13 Place du Grand Sablon*), the famous tearoom and chocolate shop. Pralines – filled chocolates – are the Belgian speciality, as well as shaped chocolates, and sculpted concoctions of chocolate and almond. Many *chocolatiers* also sell *speculoos* and other traditional sweet Belgian biscuits, *petits fours* and

confectionery intended to be eaten with coffee. These can be found at most bakers and patissiers. One traditional old bakery with an exceptional selection is Dandoy, with branches at *31 Rue au Beurre* and *14 Charles Buls,* both in the centre of Brussels. In Bruges, visit Temmerman, at Zilverpand (*63 Noordzanstraat*).

Designer clothes

Top names in new Belgian design include Kaat Tilley (*4 Galerie du Roi, Brussels*), Michel Demulder (*11–13 Rue Lepage, Brussels*), Gerald Watelet (*268 Avenue Louise, Brussels*) and Olivier Strelli (*72 Avenue Louise, Brussels*) and the radical Antwerp Six (at Stijl shops and their own stores in Antwerp).

Stijl, with several stores in rue Antoine Dansaert, Brussels, is the focal point for all interested in Belgian style – for men, women and kids. In Bruges, visit L'Heroïne, at Zilverpand in Noordzanstraat, for a choice of Belgian designers.

Antwerp continues to hold a front position for directional fashion. For the best in Belgian design trends don't miss these Antwerp addresses: Walter (*12 St Antoniusstraat*), Lieve Van Gorp (*1 Hopland*), Stephan Schneider (*53 Reynderstraat*) and Louis (*2 Lombardenvest*). For beautiful leather accessories visit

Delvaux (*17 Komedieplaats*), and for fabulous footwear from Prada and Belgian designers Demeulemeester and Bikkembergs step into Coccodrillo (*9 Schuttershofstraat*).

Diamonds and jewellery

Buy diamonds and jewellery in the diamond quarter near Antwerp's central station, or in the heart of the city around Grote Markt. Long before Antwerp, Belgium's original diamond city was Bruges, where today the Bruges Diamanthuis (*5 Cordoeanierstraat*) sells a wide selection … though one can hardly say, 'to suit all budgets'. For a look at what's happening on the modern jewellery scene, visit Christa Reniers' shop (*28 Rue du Vieux Marché aux Grains, Brussels*), or Nadine Wijnants (*26 Kloosterstraat, Antwerp*).

Lace

Elegant, intricate handmade bobbin-lace has been associated with the great Flemish towns since the Middle Ages. The modern revival of the art is much to do with tourism, but quality and skill are as high as ever. Hundreds of small shops around the main tourist sights in Brussels, Bruges, Ghent, Antwerp and Lille show what's on offer in window displays where pieces of exquisite work are pinned out to be admired. Prices are very low for this type of work, with doilies and place mats as the cheapest items. These are not mere souvenirs – buy a complete set, and they can be used at home on special occasions. More expensive items go right up to aprons, jackets, dresses and complete matching outfits. Do something extra special and buy antique lace.

Key areas to look are around Grand-Place, in the old heart of Brussels, in the upmarket central shopping areas like the Sablon, Avenue Louise and the *galeries*.

In Bruges, there's a particularly wide choice and very high quality near Burg and Markt, and along the 15-minute walk from there to the Begijnhof. A good place to buy – and watch lace being made – is at the Kantcentrum (Lace Centre) in Peperstraat (*see page 119*). There are also lace-making demonstrations at some of the shops, such as Kantjeweltje (*11 Philipstockstraat, at 1500 daily*), where a wide range of new and antique lace is for sale.

Find many little lace specialists in the centre of Ghent near the Botermarkt and Frijdagmarkt, in central Antwerp and in the old quarter of Lille.

For the authentic product, always check that lace is traditional, handmade and locally produced. Many shops display cheaper machine-made foreign lace alongside the real thing, with a lower price tag.

171

Eating out

First thing to know about Belgium is that eating and drinking are vitally important. The country has more Michelin-rated eateries per head than France. Belgians like an evening out, and for many that must include a meal. Despite that, gastronomic restaurants are far from being the usual place to eat out in Brussels. More meals are served in bars and cafés – usually warm, cosy establishments with a bar, plain wooden tables and chairs, and brisk table service. Scores of them are replete with charm and character, with big open fires, simple pre-war fixtures and fittings and waiters clad in traditional long white aprons. Many are perfect Art Nouveau museum pieces.

This unpretentious combination of bar and restaurant, similar to many French *brasseries* and British pubs, follows the style of old-fashioned *estaminets* and they are often called by that name. Customers can order anything from a coffee, beer or snack to a complete meal with salads, substantial main courses, cheeses and desserts. *Estaminet* food is generally good, served in hearty portions, and the choice of drinks includes a broad range of wines as well as a score of beers.

Street snacking

Street corner stalls called *fritures* sell filling, tasty fried snacks. A vital part of the Belgian experience

...ion of *frites* – which locals translate as Belgian, not French fries – bought and eaten in the street. Belgians are correct to consider their fries different: they are made by being fried twice, not once. Served in a cone, usually with mayonnaise, the result is delicious. A few eccentrics prefer ketchup, but fries are never eaten with vinegar. Less common than formerly, *caricoles* (sea snails), served up with their broth, are a traditional savoury stall meal. For a sweet snack, waffles and crêpes are popular. Another oily option is a freshly fried doughnut.

Brasserie favourites

The cliché that people in Belgium eat nothing but *moules frites* (mussels and fries) is actually more true of tourists. It's understandable. Where the fries and the mussels are both so good, and so cheap, it's an easy and enjoyable option at almost every inexpensive bar and café.

In addition, brasseries and bars serve a whole range of other typically Flemish dishes, and it's worth looking down the menu. Pies and savoury flans are popular on their own or as a main course. Substantial meaty and fishy stews and casseroles are classic Flemish ...ng – especially if there's a ...h of beer in the recipe. Offal is po... ...ar too, in the form of sausages, *tête pressée* (brawn) and *kipkap* (jellied meat), sometimes served with the down-to-earth *stoemp*, potato mashed with vegetables.

For quick snacks, the French classic *croque monsieur* (cheese and ham on toast) comes high on the list, along with stranger, meatier notions such as *toast cannibale* (raw minced beef on toast). Steak is a favourite, including the raw *Steak à l'américaine*.

Restaurant styles

The half-bar/half-restaurant *estaminet* style provides a relaxed ambience and a flexible approach. This informality typifies the authentic Belgian restaurant. Most 'proper' restaurants seem to be foreign. Brussels – and the other cities – have taken French cuisine

to heart, and classier eating places usually offer a French menu with French dishes.

Cheap and cheerful fish and seafood restaurants are numerous, sometimes with dinner swimming in tanks before being plucked out and rushed to the frying pan. Head away from the

173

tourist hotspots to find better dining. The best of the low-priced fish restaurants tend to be around Place Ste-Catherine in Brussels.

It's striking how many budget restaurants in central Brussels and the other Belgian cities are Greek. In second place come the Italians. Both aim for a low-budget informality, perhaps geared more to hungry visitors than locals. Spanish, Chinese, Japanese, Mexican, Indian and vegetarian restaurants and other worldwide styles can be found in all the Belgian cities.

Flemish specialities

The people of Flanders like good, hearty dishes, heavy and succulent. They like sausages (*andouilles* or *andouillettes*), tripe, pâtés, *charcuterie* and game. Fresh river and sea fish are popular too – especially if you're eating by the water.

Beer is a vital ingredient of the great Flemish stews and casseroles. The heartiest meat and veg filler is called *hochepot* (or *hotje potje*). *Waterzooi*, one of the best loved Flemish dishes, is a lighter fish soup – and also comes in a chicken version. Succulent *carbonnade flamande* is beef stewed with beer, onions, carrots and herbs. *Lapin* (rabbit) is always on the menu, again stewed or casseroled with beer and onions.

Game from the Ardennes hills in southern Belgium is of high quality, and a great favourite during autumn. Then chefs prepare their traditional dishes with wild fowl or boar, cooked with wild mushrooms.

Flamiche, a meal in itself, is a vegetable and cream tart. There's more pastry for dessert, especially fresh fruit tarts.

Beer

Let's be honest – although Belgians are the world's biggest beer drinkers, it's not all traditional Flemish beer. Interbrew and the other multinational brewing giants are here too, and do a huge trade in the country's bars. Belgian brands, such as Chimay and Hoegaarden, are readily available in the UK and other countries.

Yet Belgium does have the quirkiest, biggest, and tastiest range of traditional brews, too. There are at least 100 breweries, making over 400 kinds of beer. Few bars serve more than about 30 of these, though every town has at least one beer-lovers' bar with hundreds of varieties.

Genuine Belgian Trappist ales are made under the supervision of monks at Chimay, Orval, Rochefort, Westmalle and Westvleteren. The similar Abbey ales from the big brewers imitate the rich, dark Trappist style. These come mainly as doubel (about 6% alcohol) and tripel (about 8%).

The most distinctively Belgian brew is lambic, a naturally fermented beer. Gueuze, the speciality of Brussels, blends old and new lambics. Put in a cherry flavouring and it becomes a Kriek. Raspberry flavour makes it a Framboise.

Brand names can be whacky, like Kwak (which comes in a glass with a spherical base), Mort Subite (Sudden Death) and Guillotine. Alcohol content can be high, too – up to 9% or more, making Belgian beer as strong as wine. In winter, warm, spiced beers are available.

Other drinks

Belgian bars and cafés always have a selection of French wines. Cocktails and flavoured vodkas are popular with the younger generation. Another distinctively Belgian drink is the spirit called *genever* – or 'Dutch Gin'.

You can order a coffee in almost any bar, café or brasserie: strong and rich, it's served black with a little portion of cream and a biscuit or chocolate.

Is Lille different?

Although across the border in France, the specialities and restaurants of Lille are the same as in the rest of Belgium.

Eating times

Lunch: 1200–1400

Dinner: 1900–2200

Bars and brasseries keep long, late hours. Many are open from 0700 to 0200 the following morning. Many bars with music stay open all night.

Belgium with children

Antwerp Zoo

26 Koningen Astridplein, 2018 Antwerp. Tel: 03 202 45 40; fax 03 231 00 18. Open at 0900 daily. Closes at: Dec, Jan 1600; Feb, Oct, Nov 1630; Mar–June, Sept 1830; July, Aug 1830. Admission: ££, under 3s free. The biggest zoo in Belgium (and one of the first in Europe), is next to the railway station in the centre of Antwerp. Not especially impressive, except in size, but may hold children's attention for a while.

Aqualibi

Wavre, 1300. Tel: 010 42 16 00. Open Apr–Sept 1000–1800 Wed, Thur, Sun; 1000–2300 Fri, Sat (reserved for Walibi visitors during the day). Oct–Mar 1400–2200 Wed–Fri; 0200–2300 Sat, Sun. Admission: ££. A spacious well-equipped fun water park attached to Walibi (see page 177).

1000–1800. Admission: adults ££, children ££ (under 1m tall, free). Access: Highway E17, exit 2; A19 direction Ieper (Ypres), exit 3 to Beselare, and follow the signs of Bellewaerde Park. A popular family leisure park near Ypres.

Bellewaerde Park (Ypres)

Meenseweg, 497 B-8902 Ieper. Tel: 00 32 (57) 46 86 86; fax: 00 32 (57) 46 75 95; e-mail: info@bellewaerdepark.be Open Apr–start July 1000–1800; July–Aug 1000–1900; 1st week of Sept 1000–1800; weekends to 18 Oct

Boudenwijn Park (Bruges)

12 Avenue De Baekerstraat, St Michiels. Tel: 050 383838. Open May–Aug 1000–1800 daily. Easter, Weds and weekends in Sept, 1200–1800. Admisssion: £££. The Dolphinarium and Seal Island are the most popular attractions at this enjoyable family leisure park just south of Bruges. Other attractions include an Olympic ice rink, swimming pool, and art gallery, as well as such entertainments as a Haunted Castle, Bambinoland, a Fishing Village adventure, and a skating show called Fantasy on Ice.

Bruparck

(*See pages 80–81*). Bruparck's Mini-Europe, water park Océade, and Atomium are strongly geared to children, as well as being attractions that thrill adults at least as much as children.

Centre Belge de la Bande Déssinée (Belgian Cartoon-Strip Centre)

(*See page 52*). The Cartoon-Strip Museum has an obvious child appeal, including a children's library of comic books.

Musée de Cire (Wax Museum)

1st floor, Anspach Centre, Place de la Monnaie, 1000. Tel: 217 60 23. Open 1000–1800 daily. Admission: ££. A modest edutainment in the centre of Brussels that tells the history of the city and Flanders from Roman times.

Walibi

Wavre, 1300. 20km southeast from Brussels on A4, exit 6. By train from Brussels: from Schuman to Gare de Bierges. Tel: 010 42 15 00. Open 4 Apr–30 June 1000–1800 daily; July–18 Oct 1000–1900 daily. Admission: £££; children under 1m tall, free. Crowded, but enjoyable. Super theme park near Brussels, with brilliant rides, old-fashioned and high-tech, carefully geared to the different age groups.

After dark

Cabaret

Showpoint *14 Place Stéphanie. Tel: 02 511 5364. Open 2200–0600 Mon–Sat.* Spectacular glitz and glamour stage show. Big show nightly at midnight.

Casinos

All a flutter on the coast …
At Ostend: *Kursaal, Monacoplein. Tel: 059 705111.*
At Knokke: *509 Zeedijk-Albertstrand. Tel: 050 630500.*

Clubs and nightlife

Brussels has a thriving all-night club scene. Antwerp, Ghent and Lille also have plenty of dance venues. In central Brussels, west and south of Grand-Place is a young, late-night area with several bars and discos, though some venues open only at weekends. There's more intense, louder, more dressy clubbing at locations on the south side of the Marolles quarter. There are gay and lesbian nights at some clubs.

Two to check in Brussels:

Who's Whose Land *17 Rue Poinçon. Weekends only, 2100–0300.* Highly rated, very fashionable. Sunday night is gay.

The Fuse *208 Rue Blaes. Every Sat, right through the night 2300–0600 or later.* Huge crowds, very young. Also hosts rioutous monthly gay Démence (Sun, men) and D-Light (Fri, women).

In Bruges:

Villa Romana *1 Kraanplein. Tel: 050 34 3453. Open daily 2200–early hours.* One of the best in Bruges.

Summer festivals

Boterhammen in het park
Weekly summer rock in the royal park from end July to end Aug. Mainly Flemish.

Brosella
Easygoing free event every July in Brupark area.

Viva Brazil
Really unusual June event, a week of music as Brazil's top names descend on Brussels.

Film

Belgians love cinema, like foreign movies and fortunately prefer subtitled 'VO' (version original) to dubbed. Check which it is before you go. Top screens:

Kinepolis, Bruparck *20 Boulevard du Centenaire, Laeken. Tel: 478 0550.* Twenty-seven screens showing a wide range of films from arthouse to Disney to Hollywood.

UGC Acropole *17 Galerie de la Toison d'Or and 8 Avenue de la Toison d'Or. Tel: 0900 10440.* Eleven screens playing Hollywood favourites and arty French.

Jazz

A major attraction of Brussels (and Ghent and Antwerp) is the availability of live jazz, often in bars. Walk along Rue Antoine Dansaert or Rue Haute or around the Bourse in Brussels late at night and keep your ears open. Some principal venues in the city:

L'Archiduc *6 Rue Antoine Dansaert. Tel: 02 512 0652.* A discreet little jazz bar open afternoons till midnight, hosts frequent concerts.

Café La Pinte d'Argent *11 Place des Bienfaiteurs. Tel: 02 241 0314.* This is serious. Live jazz every day of the week, generally at 2000 (1400 on Sun), with an additional earlier gig on Wed at 1800.

New York Jazz Café *5 Chaussée de Charleroi. Tel: 02 534 8509.* A restaurant with a jazz bar, with local artists.

In Bruges, head over to **De Cactus Club** *33 St Jacobstraat* – a focal point for live jazz and rock – or **De Versteende Nacht** *11 Langestraat*, where there's often jazz playing. There's jazz in Ghent, Antwerp and other Belgian towns, and in Lille too.

Puppet theatres

Puppet theatre is a well-established and popular Belgian tradition. In Brussels: **Toone Theatre** and Museum. *End of Impasse Schuddeveld, off Petite rue des Bouchers. Tel: 02 511 71 37.*

In Ghent:
't Spelleke van de Folklore (Puppet Theatre of the Museum of Folklore) *65 Kraanlei. Tel: 09 223 13 36.*

Rock and pop

AB (Ancienne Belgique) *114 Boulevard Anspach. Tel: 02 201 5858.* Brussels' main music venue has a constant stream of big shows, and there's a first floor club for smaller gigs. The emphasis is on the Flemish community. Prices are low and the atmosphere good.

Botanique *236 Rue Royale. Tel: 02 226 6660.* Once a botanical gardens but now a major cultural venue and focal point of the Francophone community, with big rock events in the Orangerie.

Vorst Nationaal/Foret National *36 Avenue du Globe. Tel: 02 347 0355.* Huge venue for big-scale rock concerts.

Theatre, opera, dance, concerts

There's a full and dynamic programme of high-culture events, both classical and avant-garde, throughout the year. Call these major venues for information on current performances.

Cirque Royal *81 Rue de l'Enseignement. Tel: 02 218 20 15.* Not a circus, but an important location for opera, dance and concerts. Despite a rather formal, old-fashioned feel, it's also used for rock events.

Théâtre de la Monnaie/ Muntschouwburg *Entrance in Rue Léopold. Tel: 02 229 1211. Box office open 1100–1730.* Brussels' world-class opera house and home to Anne Teresa de Keersmaeker's acclaimed modern dance company Rosas.

Théâtre National de la Communauté Française de Belgique (Belgian National Theatre of the French Community) *Place Rogier, Brussels. Tel: 02 217 03 03.* French-language productions.

Koninklijke Vlaamse Schouwburg (Royal Flemish Theatre) *3 Schouwburgstraat, Ghent. Information and reservations: Tel: 09 225 24 25; website: www.vlaamseopera.be* Home of De Vlaamse Opera (The Flemish Opera Company), and venue for Flemish-language productions.

Nederlands Toneel Gent: KNS *17 Sint-Baafsplein, Ghent. Information and reservations: Tel: 09 225 32 08; website: www.ntg.be Open Mon–Sat 1100–1700. Closed on Sun and public hols.* This Ghent theatre company plays at three different locations, at this one providing simultaneous translation in English and French on Wed, Thur, Fri and Sat at 1930.

Practical
information

PRACTICAL INFORMATION

Practical information

Airports

Zaventem International Airport, 15km northeast of Brussels, is the principal airport for Brussels and the rest of Belgium. Frequent trains shuttle between airport and city in 20 minutes.

Eurostar and Thalys

Rather than fly, travellers from London and southeast England may prefer to use the high-speed Eurostar train service which gets from London Waterloo International to Brussels Midi in 2 hours 40 minutes, including the 20-minute journey through the Channel Tunnel. The train also stops at Lille Europe, 2 hours out of London.

Travellers from Paris may prefer to travel on high-speed Thalys trains,

1 hour 40 minutes from city centre (Gare du Nord) to city centre (Brussels Midi).

Climate

Mild, wet and changeable all year round, with hot, humid days in July and Aug and cool, damp days in Dec and Jan. It is rarely below freezing. Summer highs around 30°C, winter lows around 0°C.

Currency

All prices are generally shown in euros as well as national currency. Only the national currency exists in cash. Belgian money is the Belgian Franc (BEF), divided into 100 centimes. There are coins of 1/2, 1, 5, 20 and 50 francs, and notes of 100, 200, 500, 1000, 2000 and 10,000 francs.

In Lille, French money applies. The currency is the French Franc (FF), divided into 100 centimes. There are coins of $1/2$, 1, 2, 5, 10 and 20 francs, and notes at 20, 50, 100 and 200 francs.

Customs

Goods bought Duty and Tax Paid in France or Belgium can be brought into the UK without limit, if they are for personal consumption or as gifts.

Disabled travellers

La Guide Touristiques et des Loisirs, from tourist offices, contains detailed information (in French) on access to sites and other useful material for disabled people.

Electricity

The power supply in France and Belgium is 220 volts.

Entry formalities

US: No visa required. Passport with more than 3 months remaining validity.

UK: No visa required. Full 10-year passport with more than 3 months remaining validity.

Australia: No visa required. Passport with more than 3 months remaining validity.

NZ: No visa required. Passport with more than 3 months remaining validity.

Canada: No visa required. Passport with more than 3 months remaining validity.

South Africa: No visa required. Passport with more than 3 months remaining validity.

Health

It's usually possible to see a general practitioner without an appointment, or to phone to request a visit. Payment must be made on the spot. Keep doctors' and pharmacists' receipts – you will need them when claiming reimbursement, whether through Form E111 or from your travel insurance.

Information

National Tourist Offices:

France
French Tourist Office, 178 Piccadilly, London W1V 0AL. Tel: 0891 244123; fax: 0171 493 6594

Belgium
Flanders: Tourism Flanders-Brussels, 31 Pepper Street, London W14 9RW. Tel: 0171 458 0044; e-mail: info@belgium-tourism.org
Wallonia: Tourism Brussels-Ardennes, 31 Pepper Street, London W14 9RW. Tel: 0171 867 0311 (1300–1700 only); e-mail: info@belgium-tourism.orgg

Websites:

Airports
www.BrusselsAirport.be – Brussels Airport official website.

Hotels
www.resotel.be – Hotel and Services Reservation.

Museums
www.artsite.be/musea/overmus.htm – links to scores of Belgian museums on the net

Railways
www.b-rail.be – very useful and informative site of NMBS/SNCB (Belgian Railways).

www.eurostar.com – Official site of Eurostar, high-speed rail service from London to Brussels (and Paris). www.thalys.com – Official site of the Thalys high-speed service (Paris–Bruxelles–Amsterdam–Koln).

Restaurants
www.resto.be – more than 3000 Belgian restaurants.

Tickets
www.tickets.be – website of Global Tickets Belgium for online booking for rock, cultural and sports events.

Tourist offices
www.belgium-tourism.net – Belgian Tourist Office.

Other websites
www.webwatch.be/index.dlp – links to hundreds of Belgium-based websites.

Publications

Bulletin is an English-language weekly about life in Belgium for visitors and ex-pats.

What's On weekly lists events, shows, exhibitions, etc.

Both are available from tourist offices, hotels and some newsagents.

Foreign newspapers and magazines are readily available in newsagents all over the country. A wide range is on offer.

Rail information:
Tel: 02 555 2525.

Insurance

UK citizens should travel with Form E111 entitling reimbursement of part of any medical expenses incurred, as well as travel insurance covering medical emergencies.

For motorists third-party insurance is compulsory. Comprehensive insurance issued by UK insurers is valid in the EU (a Green Card is no longer required, though some insurers wish to be informed that you are going abroad).

Maps

Tourist offices have free city and country maps printed in French and Flemish. City brochures usually have a map of the city printed in the local language. *Michelin 409* covers all of Belgium in detail, and includes Lille and French Flanders.

Opening times

Shops Mostly Mon–Sat 0900–1800 or 1900. Department stores and smaller shops keep longer hours. Lunchtime closing from 1200–1400 is normal only in smaller towns, which may also have half-day closing one day per week. In tourist destinations many shops stay open on Sun.

Banks Usually Mon–Fri 0900–1600. Some close for an hour in the middle of the day.

Petrol Stations Petrol stations all over the country are open 24 hours a day, 7 days a week, though note that some are unmanned at night and require automatic credit card payment. Other petrol stations keep variable hours and may close at night or on Sundays, but as distances are short, you are unlikely to run out of petrol before finding one which is open.

Post Offices Mon–Fri 0900–1700 (a few stay open later). Sat morning only.

Tourist Offices Generally Mon–Fri 0900–1800, and also weekends from May–Oct.

Businesses Mon–Sat 0900–1800 are normal business hours, though many offices work Mon–Fri only.

Bars Mostly open 0700–2400, though many stay open later, until 0200, 0300 or even all night.

Restaurants *Estaminets* (brasseries, cafés) generally keep bar hours. Restaurants may open only at lunchtime (1200–0200) and dinner time (0700–1000).

Churches Open for visits: similar hours to museums, but tourist visits are discouraged during religious services (mostly 0830, 1030 or 1100, 1300 and 1930 on Sun, 1700 on Sat).

Museums In general, museums open 0900–1600 Tue–Sat. Most are closed Mon and public holidays. Several open for shorter hours on Sun.

Public holidays

1 Jan	New Year's Day
Mar/Apr	Easter Monday
1 May	Labour Day
8 May	VE Day
May	Ascension
May/June	Pentecost (Whit Monday)
11 July	Flemish Community Day (Belgium only)
14 July	National Day (France)
21 July	National Day (Belgium)
15 Aug	Assumption
1 Nov	All Saints
11 Nov	Armistice Day
25 Dec	Christmas

Where national holidays fall on a Sunday, the next day is taken as a holiday instead.

Reading

Charlotte Brontë Two of her lesser known novels, *Villette* and *The Professor*, are set in Brussels.

Bill Bryson The hilarious American innocent finds himself in Belgium during his European travels in *Neither Here nor There*.

William Thackeray A large part of his huge novel *Vanity Fair* is set in Brussels.

Ruth Van Waerbeek *Everybody Eats Well in Belgium* is a classic on Belgian cooking.

Tim Webb *The Good Beer Guide to Belgium and Holland*, published by the Campaign for Real Ale, tries to get a handle on this vast subject.

Pierre Wynants *Creative Belgian Cuisine* is the acclaimed cookery book by the man considered the greatest modern Belgian chef (his restaurant is Comme Chez Soi in Brussels).

And almost any Anthology of Great War Poetry, which is bound to include pieces set in Belgium, especially Ypres.

Safety and security

Ambulance or Fire Emergency
In France – dial 12
In Belgium – dial 100

Police assistance
In France – dial 17
In Belgium – dial 101

Telephones

With few exceptions, public phones in both France and Belgium require a pre-paid phone card (available from newsagents and other shops).

Directory Enquiries: 1204 or 1304 (international); 1207 or 1307 (national).

To call the UK from either country, the international dialling code is 00 44. The code for Australia is 00 61, USA and Canada 00 1, New Zealand 00 64.